Praise for *Christianity Beyond Belief*

"Here is a gentle guide at work, giving a fresh sense of how good the news is that all are invited to be the 'cooperative friends of Jesus'—living together a life of creative goodness, for the sake of others, through the power of the Holy Spirit. Hunter writes with a grace-filled hand as he sets notions of Christian life, belief, community and mission into a new imagination, a Christianity rooted in the large sweep of the biblical story and expressed in the paths of actual life. This is a seasoned voice worth listening to!"

GEORGE R. HUNSBERGER, COORDINATOR,
The Gospel and Our Culture Network, and Professor of Missiology,
Western Theological Seminary

"Todd Hunter's tenacity to purpose as an agent of Christ's kingdom, his integrity of life as a church leader, and his constancy of focus on reaching and touching lives with the love and truth of Christ—all conjoin to recommend attention to his words and work."

JACK W. HAYFORD, PRESIDENT,
International Foursquare Church, and author of Worship His Majesty

"You hold in your hands a compelling invitation to actually *experience*—not simply learn about—what it means to be a Christian and a follower of Jesus Christ. Packed with wisdom and insight from a leader who has been on the frontlines of planting, growing and leading dynamic churches across America for the past thirty years, you have here a clear and gracious presentation of life as God intends for it to be lived here and now. Whether you consider yourself a doubter, a seeker or a fully committed believer, give yourself a gift and read this book."

THE RT. REV. CHARLES H. MURPHY III,
missionary bishop and chairman of The Anglican Mission in the Americas

"I have great respect for the leadership and wisdom of Todd Hunter. This book reflects Todd's friendly spirit and down-to-earth communication style, and it also reflects Todd's radical commitment to digging deep to truly 'get' the good news of the kingdom of God. By the time you're done reading this book, you'll be immersed in one of the most important conversations taking place in the Christian community today."

BRIAN MCLAREN,
author of Finding Our Way Again

"There is a distinct yet distant drumbeat emerging in the church. It is calling Christ-followers to get in step with their Lord by going beyond simple belief into a participation *now* in the future kingdom life of the triune God, and thus to become players *now* in God's story. In *Christianity Beyond Belief,* Todd Hunter, a seasoned prophetic voice and a lover of the church, has sounded this kingdom cadence. With both clarity and passion he challenges the church, for its own good, to march to this ancient but newly emerging beat."

BERTEN A. WAGGONER,
national director, Vineyard USA

"Todd Hunter is someone who cares deeply about evangelism in contemporary culture. His huge experience in studying models of church growth give him a unique insight into this subject."

NICKY GUMBEL,
author of Questions of Life *and other Alpha books and videos*

"Todd is part of a movement to rediscover the true message of Jesus and how we are to respond to it. *Christianity Beyond Belief* is good news!"

JOHN ORTBERG,
pastor and author of The Life You've Always Wanted

"Todd Hunter has provided a concrete and practical strategy for twenty-first-century Christian living and witness. He rethinks central concepts of Christian life in terms of contemporary experience, but ties them solidly to biblical teachings and the history of Christ's people. Best of all, what he says to do is congruent with where the Holy Spirit is moving in our times and can be verified in experience. Put it to the test and you will find that a lot of 'Christian stuff' that never worked for you before actually does work. One just has to get to the reality of it, which Hunter does."

DALLAS WILLARD,
author of Hearing God

"If we truly understand that following Jesus is not about ourselves, the potential of what could happen for the gospel is absolutely incredible. But it means some very significant readjusting of the lenses of how we view our lives and the world around us. Todd lays out very practical ways of not only understanding this but actually implementing this in our lives—for the sake of others."

DAN KIMBALL,
author of They Like Jesus but Not the Church

"I thank God for *Christianity Beyond Belief.* It is an authentic witness to what life can be like when lived in the presence of Jesus . . . here . . . now. *Christianity Beyond Belief* will stir your heart, engage your mind, enlarge your soul and reshape your imagination."

RICHARD J. FOSTER,
author of Celebration of Discipline *and coauthor of* Longing for God

Todd D. Hunter

FOREWORD BY Eugene H. Peterson

Christianity
Beyond Belief

Following Jesus for the
Sake of Others

IVP Books

An imprint of InterVarsity Press
Downers Grove, Illinois

InterVarsity Press
P.O. Box 1400, Downers Grove, IL 60515-1426
World Wide Web: www.ivpress.com
E-mail: email@ivpress.com

InterVarsity Press® is the book-publishing division of InterVarsity Christian Fellowship/USA®, a movement of students and faculty active on campus at hundreds of universities, colleges and schools of nursing in the United States of America, and a member movement of the International Fellowship of Evangelical Students. For information about local and regional activities, write Public Relations Dept., InterVarsity Christian Fellowship/ USA, 6400 Schroeder Rd., P.O. Box 7895, Madison, WI 53707-7895, or visit the IVCF website at <www. intervarsity.org>.

All Scripture quotations, unless otherwise indicated, are taken from the The Message. *Copyright © 1993, 1994, 1995, 1996, 2000, 2001, 2002. Used by permission of NavPress Publishing Group. All rights reserved.*

Published in cooperation with Kathryn Helmers of the Creative Trust Agency, Nashville, Tennessee.

Design: Cindy Kiple
Images: Irina Tischenko/iStockphoto

ISBN 978-0-8308-3256-9

Printed in the United States of America ∞

Library of Congress Cataloging-in-Publication Data

Hunter, Todd D., 1956-
  Christianity beyond belief: following Jesus for the sake of others
  /Todd D. Hunter.
     p. cm.
  Includes bibliographical references.
  ISBN 978-8308-3315-3 (cloth: alk. paper)
  1. Christian life. I. Title.
  BV4501.3.H865 2009
  248.4—dc22

                                                                    2008039550

P	18	17	16	15	14	13	12	11	10	9	8	7	6	5	4	3	2	1
Y	25	24	23	22	21	20	19	18	17	16	15	14	13	12	11	10			

CONTENTS

Foreword by Eugene Peterson 9

Acknowledgments. 13

PART ONE: A NEW UNDERSTANDING OF WHAT IT MEANS
        TO BE A CHRISTIAN

1 What If You Knew You Were Going to Live Tomorrow?
  The Problem with Getting "Saved" 17

2 Jesus' Surprising Gospel
  It's the Kingdom Now, Not Just Heaven Later 33

3 It's Our Life That Counts
  Aligning with God's Story 49

4 The Role of the Church
  Jesus Is Not Just Your Personal Savior 63

PART TWO: A NEW WAY TO LIVE

5 Cooperative Friends of Jesus
  Maybe Jesus Didn't Intend to Start a World Religion 75

6 Consistent Lives of Creative Goodness
  Apologetics of Another Kind 93

7 For the Sake of Others
  Jesus Could Have Done Backflips on a Donkey 109

8 Through the Power of the Holy Spirit
    No Big Hair, No Bizarre Behavior, Just Power for a Purpose 127

9 Inviting Others to Live a New Way
    A Fresh Approach to Sharing Our Faith 143

10 Three Is Enough Groups
    A New Way to Live 157

Appendix 1—Triads: The Theoretical Basis
    for Three Is Enough Groups 173

Appendix 2—The Person and Work of the Holy Spirit 179

Appendix 3—*The Message:* A New Testament Tour of Life . . . 185

Notes 195

Debbie

I learn love and life from you

and

Jonathan and Carol

Being your father is way better than anything I do

FOREWORD

We live in a country that is becoming less Christian by the day. People who make a living compiling statistics on these kinds of things tell us that we have an epidemic of people leaving the church. Recently I was told that one of these pollsters has concluded that nonbelievers are the fastest growing "faith" group in America. The alarm has been sounded and panic is widespread. There is considerable finger-pointing at the failure of the church to stanch the hemorrhage of membership.

Todd Hunter is not one of them. Todd Hunter has been intimately involved in the American church scene for thirty years now. He has experienced the good, the bad and the indifferent from the inside. He hasn't wasted even as much as ten minutes of those thirty years as a spectator criticizing or kibitzing from the sidelines. He knows the American church world firsthand and in detail. He is not alarmed. "Nothing was ever accomplished in a stampede" (von Hugel). I detect no hint of panic.

What he has done is give careful attention to what is going on in American culture these days, accept it without complaint as his congregation, and work out ways of living, talking about and inviting others to enter into what God is doing in this kingdom-of-God world that has been given to us. He doesn't bash the churches. He doesn't attack the so-called postmodern age as the enemy. He embraces the huge gospel announcement that the kingdom Jesus announced is, in fact, at hand (and has been "at hand" for a long time) and God is at work in daily life, real life. Quietly and without fanfare he tells us how and why he is choosing to live his life as "a cooperative friend of Jesus."

This is refreshing, this quiet voice. There is urgency conveyed in these pages, certainly, but not desperation. There is no business-as-usual complacency in his approach, but a carefully thought out and practiced engagement with men and women conversationally on their terms.

And story. This book gives us a thorough reorientation in story as the comprehensive way to understand and experience the following of Jesus. We have all grown up in an American culture that "knew not Joseph." We live in a world of information and news. We learn to think and feel and use language in Flip Wilson's "church of what's happening now." Verbally pummeled by disconnected and random things and events, facts and ideas, but increasingly hungry for a story into which we can live, find a plot, experience relationships, explore meaning. Story—the Jesus story, the king story, my story—takes priority over information or argument in the way we go about following Jesus and talking to others about following Jesus. Hunter reorders our imaginations to give priority to living in relationship with others and with God. Doctrines and morals are still important, but if there is not story, there is no relationship, no plot, no named people to love and serve.

When we depersonalize the gospel into concepts or institutionalize it into a collective identity or program it into a good cause or individualize it into a ticket into heaven, we suck the life out of it. Todd Hunter recovers the large, capacious, biblically storied context for us so that we can live *biblically*—in his words, as "cooperative friends of Jesus, in creative goodness, for the sake of others, through the power of the Holy Spirit."

Martin Thornton, a man from whom I learned much, wrote that when he finished reading a book he would flip back through the pages and find YBH scribbled on many of the margins: *Yes, but how?* "Won-

derful ideas, great sentences, moving expositions. Yes, but how?" I
think I can assure you that when you come to the end of this book
there will not be a single "Wonderful ideas, great sentences, moving
expositions. Yes, but how?" I think I can assure you that when you
come to the end of this book there will not be a single YBH in the
margins. And why? Because Todd Hunter provides a simple but stra-
tegic *how* for maintaining and practicing the integrity of the Christian
life in the real-life places where we spend most of our time in the particular cultural conditions handed to us by postmodern America. He
names the *how* "Three Is Enough." I will let him tell you how it works.
Read with expectation.

Eugene Peterson
Professor Emeritus of Spiritual Theology
Regent College, Vancouver, B.C.

ACKNOWLEDGMENTS

I am the product of my teachers. Being a lifelong, avid learner and highly curious person, I am aware I have probably never had an original thought. I happily claim indebtedness to Greg Laurie and Chuck Smith of the Calvary Chapel movement. They taught me to love and study the Bible. They modeled the value and practice of connecting with outsiders who were searching for God. John Wimber and the Vineyard were a huge influence on my life in terms of learning to lead others while simultaneously taking the faith-filled risks associated with following the leadership of the Holy Spirit.

Later, people like Richard Foster, Dallas Willard, Eugene Peterson and Elizabeth O'Connor taught me that there is an indispensable and beautiful inner journey in following Jesus. From them I learned that my ability to lead, follow the Spirit and connect in healing ways with others was directly tied to what was happening spiritually in me.

Recently I have benefited from the work of the British missionary and theologian Lesslie Newbigin, and the authors associated with the Gospel and Our Culture Network. They have shown me that all the elements of my life—the Bible, leadership, the Holy Spirit, spiritual transformation—derive their most profound meaning in a missional, serving and others-focused engagement with the people and routines of my everyday life.

My students have also taught me a great deal. Teaching and lecturing in seminaries and coaching young Christian leaders have provided insights about relationships, community and truth-seeking that I could not have grasped in any other way. From them I learned that the fear-based Christian pundits are wrong. For all the possible flaws in the postmodern, post-Christian world, I see in these young leaders an engagement with their culture that is decidedly Jesus-centered and effective. They have eyes for opportunity in our "post" society. They see that many people are postsecular, which means they believe that the material world is the only reality. These people are very open to hearing about spirituality—the way of Jesus—when we relate to them on their terms.

Finally, British theologian N. T. Wright has pulled all these strands together by explaining the Bible, "from Genesis to the maps," as a coherent story. Wright recounts a full-bodied narrative that connects the aims and purposes of God from precreation intentionality to the bursting newness of God's completed story in the renewed heaven and earth. This is a real gift to the practice of evangelism and discipleship in our times. Wright invites us to participate in, do incarnational ministry with and align ourselves to God's story. In my view, acting in that story is what it means to be a Christian. It is what Jesus died for. While heaven is the destination of these "actors," spiritual transformation into the cooperative people of God is the goal.

While I am genuinely indebted to these leaders and to others too numerous to name, the faults in my thinking or writing are mine. I certainly do not deserve any special attention for conveying the ideas in this book. I stand on the shoulders of others.

Anne Lamott's book on writing, *Bird by Bird*, has a chapter on being willing to write poor first drafts. I think I've made this an art form! Kathryn Helmers, my agent, and Cindy Bunch, my editor at InterVarsity Press, took my cobbled-together ideas and shaped them into this book. I cannot thank them and the entire team at IVP enough. They deserve huge credit for any good this book ends up doing.

PART ONE

A New Understanding of
What It Means to Be a Christian

WHAT IF YOU KNEW YOU WERE GOING TO LIVE TOMORROW?

The Problem with Getting "Saved"

Because Jesus was raised from the dead, we've been given a brand-new life and have everything to live for, including a future in heaven—and the future starts now! . . . As obedient children, let yourselves be pulled into a way of life shaped by God's life, a life energetic and blazing with holiness. . . . Your life is a journey you must travel with a deep consciousness of God.

1 PETER 1:3-4, 14, 18

When I was a teenager in middle-class Santa Ana, California, my peers tended to fall into one of two categories. My honest, though admittedly dim, memory is that we tended to be pursuing either (1) sex, drugs and rock 'n' roll, or (2) Jesus. I know because I lived my rebellious teen years in the cradle of the Jesus Movement. In high school my friends were converting to Christ at what I thought was a troubling and disquieting rate. They were listening to Jesus music and watching Jesus movies in a tent at a place called Calvary Chapel, which was on the border of Santa Ana and Costa Mesa. Though I was somewhat culturally religious, I just couldn't see why anyone would give up sex, drugs or rock for Jesus and his music.

In the early 1970s one of the most well-known bumper stickers on the VWs in Orange County was "JESUS LIVES!" I'd see it daily, and some days I wondered, *What does it mean that Jesus lives? In what sense? No one says they see him walking the streets. In what manner does he live? Does he have a body, or what?*

At times, perhaps in more reflective moments, I wondered, *If Jesus does live, what difference does it make to me? How would his living today make a difference to me?* As 1 Peter 1 states, I wondered, *How might Jesus' present life pull me into a new way of life?* I had some knowledge of Jesus' virgin birth, death and resurrection, but I couldn't wrap my head around the importance of Jesus being alive today. Some of the young converts around me seemed to be changed by the idea that Jesus rose from the dead. But still I wondered how that bit of historical information, so central to Christian thought, might draw me into a new way of life. I didn't think about it much, but when I did, I figured, intuitively, that Jesus' "now" life had to be about more than something he said or did thousands of years ago.

FINDING A LIFE WORTH LIVING

My adolescence was shaped by a singular event: the death of my older brother, Dennis, in Vietnam. Thinking back, I remember that the "conflict" in Vietnam hung over U.S. culture like the deep fog that sometimes envelops coastal Southern California. It was hard to see where the world was headed. At the time I was clueless about most of this—after all, I had Pony League Baseball games and not getting caught for "this and that" to worry about.

My life was interrupted on a typically great-weather spring Saturday in 1969. The world seemed good to a naive thirteen-year-old boy. There was lots of excited talk of men walking on the moon, Woodstock marked a whole generation, the movie *Midnight Cowboy* was worrying many people, and *Butch Cassidy and the Sundance Kid* entertained me and my friends. Best of all, to my mind, a small circus had come to town and was set up a couple of blocks from my home.

As I'd soon come to see, this was also to become the strangest and most tragic of all childhood days. Innocent and in pursuit of simple fun, I left home to walk to the circus, gawking at the various acts. Little did I know that while I was viewing one spectacle, a scene of another sort had broken out at my house. Innocence was soon to be lost.

Leaving the circus and walking a block or so up our typical tree-lined street, I could see that our driveway and both sides of the street in front of our yellow, shrub-fronted house was packed with cars. It looked like a neighbor was having a birthday party or something. But the crowd was at *my* house. And it wasn't a party—no one was laughing. They were crying. Crying doesn't do justice to how I remember my mom. I remember something more like the phrase from the Bible: "unspeakable yearning, wordless moans and groaning heartache too deep for utterance."

But what do you expect from a mother who has just heard that her beloved son has been killed and that "we'll be sending home as much of his body as we can"? *As much of his body!* How do you process that? I wonder if she pictured his little hands playing with toys, or his greasy hands working on a '56 Chevy? Just what parts would be coming home?

I think I was stunned into an emotional shutdown that, to some degree, I have had to fight my way out of ever since. I have no clear memory of how I felt at the moment I walked through the front door. It all hit me later. I remember being somewhere—it seems to me it was a military base—and hearing a commendation read of my brother. He had been awarded the bronze and silver stars for bravery in battle. The commendation said something very close to this: "Corporal Hunter left the safety of his foxhole to engage the enemy in a crossfire. In so doing he saved many men. In this selfless action he was hit by a mortar shell and killed."

I remember thinking in my crude way: *That's the biggest bunch of bull I've ever heard in my life!* He had only been there a few weeks. Why would the same guy who, on the one hand, used to beat on me in the backyard—me, his brother—on the other hand, *die* for a bunch of guys he hardly knew? And for a cause the nightly news said was a waste?

I was really angry and confused. For months or years, I can't remember, I had recurring dreams of sneaking off to Vietnam to kill "those gooks," as they were nastily labeled in those days, those people who killed my brother. In my dreams I hid away in a plane to sneak over to Vietnam; others times my hideaway was a boat. I don't remember ever getting there, in my dreams, and actually pulling it off. The dreams always ended in frustration. This time of intense, bitter and perplexing resentment hit its peak, in all places, in the courtyard of a typical little Methodist church, which my family attended. The people of the church had decided to give tribute to my brother by erecting a flagpole in his honor in the grassy area of the courtyard.

If hearing the commendation read at the military base was a trigger, seeing the unveiled plaque on the flagpole set a bomb off in me. The commemorative inscription said in part: "Greater love hath no man than this, that [he] lay down his life for his friends." I remember thinking, *Oh great, now they are bringing God into it, as if he had anything to do with it!* I remember, deep within myself, cursing the idea that there was anything worth dying for—especially for what, to my naive young mind, was a stupid war. I remember saying to God, *I don't believe this. I don't believe you; I don't believe you have anything to do with this or any part of these horrible circumstances.* I think my inward response was actually a lot worse than that. I know it was really bad, but the memories have faded.

I don't recall hearing any clear response from God, just a gracious silence. In hindsight I think the grace must have been mixed with a big dose of understanding. I recollect walking from the ceremony with the uneasy feeling that I had not succeeded in putting God in his place.

I remember thinking that the episode was probably not the end of a conversation that had begun with God.

The next big episode came about six years later. By now it was 1976 and I was nineteen, playing baseball in college. A player on the team repeatedly asked me to go to church with him. He said the music would be cool. He bugged me about it so much that I finally said to Debbie, my then girlfriend, now my wife, "Oh let's just go. What can happen at church?"

My friend was right; the music was cool. The message was simple, clear and Bible-based, easy for a nineteen-year-old to understand. At the end of the talk an invitation was given to raise our hands if we wanted to respond to what we had just heard, to become a follower of Jesus.

The pews in this church were packed with young people. Built to seat eight, each pew had at least ten crammed in. In fact, people were sitting on the floor and in folding chairs outside. Debbie and I were so close together that I could notice when she twitched a muscle. I was really paying attention, because I wanted to feel if she raised her hand. She didn't, and neither did I. A moment later the people who raised their hands were asked to come to the front of the church "to give your life to Jesus." Neither of us went forward, but something happened that night. Debbie and I talked about it on the way back from church.

The next morning I bumped into my friend at the baseball office. I told him that something had happened to me that I couldn't understand or explain, but that I wanted to go back to church the next Sunday and go forward like other people had done. Debbie and I went back the next week and experienced the exact same routine: cool music, easily understood message and an invitation to become followers of Jesus. This time we both raised our hands and walked to the altar. In fact, we leaped up. We were the first to the front of the church, standing right in front of the pulpit.

As the evangelist began to lead us in a prayer, asking for forgiveness and committing our lives to God, the whole episode of my brother came flashing into my mind. I heard the God I had yelled at six years ago say to me: "Todd, this is it. This is what is worth laying down your life for—to follow me for the sake of others as your brother followed his instinct to rescue his trapped comrades." Along this path, I was led to believe, I would find the real and everlasting life. In that moment I knew that Jesus did in fact live, as the bumper stickers and my friends attested. He lived and lives the most compelling and interesting life imaginable. His life, life in the kingdom as the Son of God, is our model for eternal life.

CHRISTIANITY IS A LIFE

I've arranged this book in two parts so we—writer with reader—can stay connected. In this first section I'll suggest a new understanding of what it means to be a Christian. In part two I'll set forth a way of doing life connected with this new understanding. Reading what I've just typed sounds like it could be overreaching—maybe even naive. I think we are safe, however. I know that I'm not saying anything new. Frankly, that would be too bold for me! But I also know that what we are about to consider together will sound new to many of you. Nevertheless this is, in my opinion, a point of view worth considering. I know it has been good for me and thousands of others I have known.

Somehow, in the years after the dramatic events surrounding the death of my brother and my conversion, I became drastically inconsistent. I was a backward or reverse hypocrite. Instead of preaching more than I was living, I was living more than my preaching communicated. I was living an amazing and exciting spiritual adventure, full of risk and growth and religious escapades. But in hindsight, my explanation of the gospel was shriveled. I used to think that eternal life was what we got after we died. (Today, I know better—new life, a different kind of life, *starts* at conversion and it *never ends*.)

I am not sure how this inadvertent, two-faced disconnect got such a foothold in my life. Perhaps it has to do with the environments in which I was converted and lived my earliest days as a Christian. They were marked by an amazing presence of God. Literally every Sunday dozens of young people my age were turning to faith. The Bible teaching was startling in its simplicity and power. It was clear that many people were having authentic, undeniable interactions with the Holy Spirit. The gifts of the Spirit were flowing, people were being healed, others were delivered from drug addictions, families were being put back together, and messed-up teenagers were giving up patterns of sin.

Looking back, it seems like I was living in a remarkable bubble. But at some point the bubble burst. It may have burst on the pin of ignorance—a simple lack of knowledge. Imagine that the first people to make and experience the benefits of fire didn't realize that sparks from the stones they struck together had started the kindling glowing? I think something like that was going on in our lives. We experienced huge benefits, but either we never thought about the reason, or we thought about it in ways that sabotaged us in the long term.

After decades of being a follower of Jesus and a pastor, I recognize at least one place I went wrong. As 1 Peter 1 says, Christianity is about "a brand-new life." This new life does indeed have an unspeakably marvelous future. But that future starts *now*. Though we were catching glimpses of the future in our present lives, because of our lack of knowledge our focus was still mostly on the life to come. Our ignorance reminds me of when Paul asks some people in Ephesus if they received the Holy Spirit when they believed. They reply that they had not even heard of the Holy Spirit (Acts 19:1-2). In parallel maybe we would have said, "Eternal life in this life? No, we have never even heard of it."

Yet that is exactly what Christianity is about: a certain kind of life—eternal life. It is about living in alliance with the gospel Jesus

announced concerning the kingdom of God. Or as Peter says, it is a
"way of life shaped by God's life." Christianity is a journey: following
Jesus' model of life in the kingdom through the power of the Holy
Spirit in the actual events of our lives.

But this kind of followership cannot happen when our imaginations* are shaped by the notion that eternal life is "out there, somewhere beyond the stars, after I die." Nor is it merely about length of
life or ongoing existence. Even dead things can continue to exist—
just look out the window. I'll bet you'll see a dead plant, tree or weed
that keeps "existing."

I think you'll agree with me that mere existence is not what God
intends by eternal life. Rather than being spatial or chronological,
eternal life is qualitative. It is a different kind of life. Peter says, "Your
new life is not like your old life" (1 Peter 1:23). Eternal life is a special
quality of life. Though this new kind of life affects the afterlife, it cannot be reduced to it. It's something new that replaces the old.

The clearest statement in the Scripture regarding eternal life
shows it is fundamentally about a type of life. In John 17:3, Jesus says
that eternal life is knowledge of God and his Son. As important as
good thinking is, the knowledge Jesus refers to is not merely thinking about or mental agreement with a certain set of doctrines. Eternal life is the quality life derived from and lived within the kingdom
of God. It is personal, intimate community with the Trinity. It is
the kind of life, which was lost due to sin, that God always intended
for humanity. In fact, sin is the counterintention of humans to live

---

*I use the term *imagination* frequently in this book. I do so because I am convinced
that people live from their imaginations, not from facts or data, as important as
they are. A young girl spends hours practicing before a mirror, checking her pos-
ture and so forth, because she has a vision of—imagines—being on the silver
screen. We know the same pattern hold true for athletes. I don't read the Bible to
merely gather facts, though they are there. I read it to shape my imagination about
what it means to be a follower of Jesus.

outside of God's story, outside of a new kind of life.

Most people who realize that Jesus lives *experience* it before they grasp it as a true idea. Though doctrine is important for other reasons, we don't need a perfect understanding of the incarnation or the atonement to experience God's gift of eternal life. Something better and more life-shaping is available: a rock-solid knowledge that you have interacted with Jesus, that you have felt his presence and heard his voice in a way that is real to you. His presence and voice are creative. They inaugurate and sustain a new kind of life—eternal life.

That Christianity is about a new, creative and eternal kind of life is crucial and brightly illuminating. As we move through the remaining chapters of this book, I hope this idea will move you to ask a few revealing questions that have been helpful to me as I've processed the notion of Christianity as "a brand-new life . . . that starts now . . . and is lived in deep consciousness of God" (1 Peter 1). Presently, as I think about how best to express Christianity, I think of these questions:

- If we knew we were going to live tomorrow and for a long time thereafter, if we believed we were eternal beings by nature, what would we do?

- Who would we follow?

- Around what narrative would we organize the various aspects of our life?

As we answer these questions, we determine the kind of life we will live. We decide the kind of persons we will become eternally. These questions lead us beyond wondering where we go when we die. They lead us to a life that never ends—not even death can kill life in Jesus' kingdom.

The Problem with Getting "Saved"

Every seat in the arena was full, the place was buzzing with anticipation. The crowd had experienced a full night of music. They heard a message designed to convince them that they were sinners in the eyes of God. The preacher explained the importance of having our sins forgiven so that we would be accepted by God into heaven. Testimonials were presented about the effects of "inviting Jesus into your heart." Everyone knew the crucial moment had come as the evangelist neared the big emotional crescendo of his sermon and the altar call: "Is your eternal destiny secure? If you walked out of here tonight and got ran over by truck and killed, do you know where you would go? Would you go to heaven or hell?"

I'm not picking on anybody with this stereotypical sound bite. I've said words to that effect hundreds of times in my life. I bring it up to help us start thinking about the nature of Christian life. It seems to me that many Christians have been imagining the wrong story concerning God and his people, and thus they come up with less-than-helpful ways of thinking about the Christian life.

The story these sound bites lead to is one in which the forgiveness of sin is the sole plot line. The plot line moves toward the final resolution of "who goes to heaven and who goes to hell." Those bumper-sticker bits of theology say that the only essential thing happening between God and humans is mere forgiveness. Let's stop and think about these simple and common ways of explaining Christianity.

Here is the first problem: that story very rarely produces actual *followers* of Jesus. At best it produces "forgiven people"—and even then I think forgiveness is only understood in a very shallow way. I believe that in responding to Jesus, people do not merely receive forgiveness of sins so they can go to heaven. Rather, they are forgiven so they can begin a different kind of life, a cooperative relationship with God, a new and eternal kind of life right now (which ultimately includes heaven).

But if the gospel and eternal life have to do with our life on earth, maybe we have misunderstood even basic terms like *sin*. Perhaps the issue in the Garden of Eden was not *sin* as we usually think about it—sex, alcohol, drugs or forbidden fruit, and popular media's exploitation of them. I think the issue may have been more about sin as rebellion; at issue is a decision to take the first step on a path away from God—to try to become our own god. To sin in biblical terms means "to miss the mark" (God's bulls-eye), "to go your own way," "to take the wrong road," "defiance of (God's) intention," "to stray from the correct path." It means to ignore or fight against God's story and his intention for us.

Those definitions alert us that there is a lot more going on in God's story than just forgiving or punishing sins. God really wants us to become his cooperative friends and co-laborers—working with God in the routines of our new life. Far from trying to make forgiveness less important in the Christian story, my aim is to show that understanding sin in the context of God's story is crucial to forming a new life, a cooperative friendship with God. I want us to see forgiveness as a starting line, a threshold to a new, fully human life. In my experience, forgiveness is often viewed as a finishing line, with a "whew" and a wipe of the brow while thinking *I'm in.* I have no quarrel with the notion that forgiveness gets us in. But I want to emphasize that it gets us into a new life story, not merely into heaven when we die.

The new life story God is writing for us is this: he intends to have a people on earth who happily, easily and routinely embody, announce, and demonstrate the rule and reign of his kingdom. Failing to value this overarching story, this wider context, is what betrays most of our thinking about what it means to be a Christian.

As you've undoubtedly heard, context is pivotal. "Hit the bat" means one thing on a baseball diamond but something entirely different in the flying mammals section of the zoo. "I'm saved" means one thing in the context of a story about "going to heaven when you die." It means something completely different in the eternal drama in which we are invited, as followers of Jesus, to live on earth under the rule and reign of God (and later go to heaven).

Picture this common scene: Your father asks you to do a few chores after you get home from school one Friday afternoon. He and Mom are working until 5 p.m. and special dinner guests will be arriving at 6. Dad is counting on your faithfulness in order to achieve his goal of hosting and serving others. But as you get a ride home from school that Friday, someone suggests a quick trip to the mall. Because you'd like something new to wear to the game that night, you agree to go. On the way home—at 5:30—you remember your father's request, which you had agreed to.

Of course when you see your father, he doesn't even have to say anything; you see disappointment and anger on his face. You apologize, he forgives you, and his face changes. But his goal is not accomplished merely in your act of sorrow and regret, and his forgiveness. People are still coming to dinner; the dining room still needs to be picked up and vacuumed, the good dishes need to be fetched from the china hutch, the table set, and so on.

That kind of cooperative father-child relationship is the will (goal) of God. He desires to have a renewed humanity who participates in his plan to restore creation. God's story cannot be reduced merely to the forgiveness of sins. Yes, sin is a big part of the divine-human story, but sin and forgiveness are not the whole story, which is about being the cooperative friends of Jesus, creatively seeking to do good for the sake of others through the power of the Holy Spirit.

You will read these four phrases throughout this book:

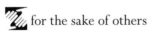 cooperative friends of Jesus

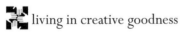 living in creative goodness

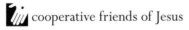 for the sake of others

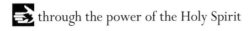 through the power of the Holy Spirit

For me these are something like a new "Four Spiritual Laws"—a brief, four-pronged way of introducing someone to what it means to be a Christian. Once people catch that vision and begin to follow Jesus, all the rest will come into play: sin, grace, forgiveness, repentance, the cross, resurrection and so forth. We can't go down the path marked by these four phrases without all of orthodox Christian teaching coming into view. I am indebted to Dallas Willard for the first two phrases. I have mulled over these two phrases—and the two I added—and spoken to others about them for ten years now. They have not let me down. They have the potential to shape a person's imagination—inspired, gifted and animated by the Holy Spirit—for following Jesus, leading to living a life of creative goodness for the sake of others.

MADE, MARRED AND MENDED

I hope by now you will agree that there is more going on in the Christian story than the often-seen bumper-sticker claim of "Just Forgiven." We need an image for how to move beyond forgiveness. Think of a thermometer: negative numbers on the bottom half, zero in the middle and positive numbers on the top half. We all come to God starting below zero, in debt. Contemporary Christians are pretty clear about how our negatives or demerits are taken care of—justification by faith, which is a gracious gift of God.

But how do we move from zeroed accounts, which allow entrance into heaven, to the positive lifestyle of following Jesus? Contemporary Christians, who are often ensnared by fear of works, legalism or religiosity, have a hard time imagining this. (It's been humorously asserted that all Christians are saved by grace, and many of us are paralyzed by it as well!) We carry on the same way we got in—through unmerited grace and through the power of the Holy Spirit, another gracious gift. But we must be clear here; there is something for Christians to do—to faithfully embody the kingdom story of God. This involves cooperation, but it does not earn salvation.

Perhaps a rhetorical question would help clear our thinking: Who do you suppose appropriates more grace in a God-honoring way: someone who merely experiences forgiveness, or someone like the apostle Paul, who said, "I worked harder than anyone, but it wasn't me; it was the grace of God in me" (1 Corinthians 15:10, my paraphrase). Think too of Paul's famous words in Philippians that he regarded all things as loss because of the overarching value of following Jesus (Philippians 3:7). Was Paul confused about what it meant to be a Christian? Was he trying to earn his way into heaven by such focused and passionate behavior? Or was he, as I suggest, in the grip of a story that had shaped both his imagination and behavior?

I've long been a fan of Billy Graham. I used to collect Graham's sermons. One in particular set forward his vision of God's intention for Christians. It gives us a rationale for moving beyond mere forgiveness. It is titled "Made, Marred and Mended."

In my recollection, the sermon showed why God *made* humans in the first place—to be his cooperative friends, working with him to redeem the earth and its people—both in this life and in the age to come. But this God-imaged, agape-based "doing good for others" objective is *marred* by rebellion, self-will and all manner of sin. God then *mends* us. This starts with leading us, by grace, to repentance and forgiving us of our sins. But it only starts there. Having sin-fixed humans was not God's original motivation for creating, nor was it his ultimate intention for humankind. This is obviously true. Sin came after God asked humans to be his cooperative friends (Genesis 2–3). Rather, we are mended so that we can get back in the game of life as God's cooperative friends.

If being mended to live in the plan of God is the main objective of Christianity, then what about heaven and hell in a story that goes beyond sound-bite, bumper-sticker theology? If what I have said so far is true, can you see how heaven and hell, while real, are not the most important points? Here is a subversive but illuminating thought:

What if the function of heaven in the biblical story is destination, not goal? The goal of Christianity is not arriving in heaven upon death. The goal is spiritual transformation into Christlikeness. That makes heaven simply the destination of God's cooperative friends, the people who love him and what he is up to on the earth. Hell then is just the opposite, a cosmic place for those who want nothing to do with God or his plan, will, story and intention.

Rapture or Revolution?

As a young Christian I didn't think much of this life mattered. I was just waiting for the rapture—the snatching up of God's people to heaven before the Great Tribulation—the time of worldwide trouble. I take responsibility for this. I don't blame any of my early teachers. But here is the deal: it doesn't make sense to pursue spiritual transformation for the sake of being God's cooperative friends when the only things that matter are associated with the life to come.

The unfolding of my life—a wife, kids, a home—began to soften those views. Later, as I began to think seriously about these things, I discovered the message of Jesus—the good news of new life in God's kingdom. Thinking through the implication of what Jesus said, not just what is said about him in the rest of the Bible, is both surprising and a launching pad for a new kind of life. And so we turn now to the astounding message of the gospel.

For Reflection and Discussion

1. Thinking of the story in the beginning of the chapter, have you had an experience that led you to a "this is what life is all about" moment? If so, what was it for you?

2. This chapter argues that Christianity is about life, not just an eternally secure death. What would you do if you knew you were going to live tomorrow and for a long time after?

Who would you follow in order to learn to really live? Why?

3. What do you make of the definition of eternal life in this chapter? How might it inform your view of what it means to be a Christian?

4. What are we saved from? What are we saved to?

How might rethinking these questions on the basis of "Made, Marred and Mended" lead to a new way of articulating what it means to be a Christian?

JESUS' SURPRISING GOSPEL

It's the Kingdom Now,
Not Just Heaven Later

The gospel is not just a message to be proclaimed;
it is the form of our participation in what God is doing in and for the world.

FROM *STORM FRONT: THE GOOD NEWS OF GOD*

About a decade ago I had a momentous lunch with philospher and writer Dallas Willard in a Mexican restaurant across the street from his office at The University of Southern California. Growing up a UCLA fan, wearing blue and gold any time I could, it was hard to be around so much cardinal and gold. But being with Dallas is worth almost any price!

I met Dallas through a mutual pastor friend. I wanted to get to know him for several reasons. I valued his work on spiritual formation. I knew we shared a real connection regarding the kingdom of God. I also needed his help with the truth-oriented issues arising within postmodernism. The agenda for this particular lunch, as I recall, was the nature of truth and how it works with notions of faith, certainty, the reliability of Scripture and so forth.

As we settled into the restaurant booth, we caught up on personal news and engaged in a little small talk while munching on chips and salsa. Because my mentor, John Wimber, had recently died, and because Dallas had admired John's relentless but childlike pursuit of life in the kingdom, we got onto the topic of the kingdom of God. I can't remember precisely what Dallas said about the centrality of Jesus' announcement of the kingdom, but I do recall saying in response, "That changes everything!"

Dallas, seeing that he had rocked my world and being the kind and empathetic man he is, gently put his hand on my forearm and said something like "Now just relax, Todd." But I couldn't relax then, and I haven't been able to get it out of my mind in the ensuing years. I am a learner-activist. When I can see something is important and true, I have a powerful inner drive to implement it immediately. I'm not saying the drive is all good. I'm just coming clean; it's there!

That conversation was like fanning the smoldering embers of an old fire, one that still has the potential to burn hot even though the embers appear dead. I wasn't hearing about the kingdom for the first time; I had heard Wimber teach on it many times. Nevertheless, something in my conversation with Dallas made me dive back in to what Jesus said about the gospel. I was desperate to figure out, from Jesus' words, what it means to be a Christian. I wanted to connect Christianity more to "what I would do if I knew I was going to live."

REDISCOVERING THE GOSPEL

The gospel is "of God." I plunged in at Mark 1:14-15, making mental notes as I went along in the brief passage: After John was put in prison, Jesus went into Galilee, proclaiming the good news of God. "The time has come," he said. "The kingdom of God is near. Repent and believe the good news!" (NIV). Let's analyze this.

The first thing to note is that the gospel is not all about us. It's about God. It first concerns God—his plan, his will and his agenda for creation. The good news originates in and springs from God. God is its initiator and he performs his plan to perfection. The gospel is about

God's unfailing plan for humanity. It isn't another consumer item to acquire, securing us a blissful happily-ever-after eternity, but the present reality of the kingdom—the rule and reign—of God through faith in Jesus that leads to following him.

Our story does not start with us and our need. It doesn't start with our sin, mistakes and imperfections and then look forward to heaven. It starts with the perfect intention of God to have a people who love him and work with him for the sake of others. Our story looks backward first. It moves from God's work with Adam and Eve to Abraham, Moses, Ruth, David, the prophets, John the Baptist, Mary, Jesus and finally to the renewed people of God. It looks forward to God's perfection in the new heaven and the new earth.

The time has come. I take this phrase to mean something like "all the events and people related to the ground work have taken their place and done their jobs. Now . . ." This phrase both grounds the announcement in the unfolding story of God and draws attention to its *kairos* element. The Greek word *kairos*—meaning a special point in time—underlines the fact that Jesus' announcement was the pivotal moment in human history. The kingdom was invading human reality in an entirely new way through Jesus. The phrase ties God's story together: past, current in-breaking of his kingdom, and the ultimate fulfillment that it assures.

The kingdom of God is near. The kingdom of God is best thought of as the rule and reign of God. It is the expression of his will. If we think of the Lord's Prayer in this context, "your kingdom come, your will be done on earth as it is in heaven," then we can see that the kingdom is the realm in which what God wants is actually done. In the person, words and works of Jesus this reality has come near. Maybe even closer than any time since the first humans were banished from the Garden of Eden. For some, I think, this is a little bit of a downer when compared to "going to heaven." But Jesus thought it was the best and greatest news anyone could ever hear.

HOW DO WE RESPOND TO JESUS' GOSPEL?

Jesus gave us two directives for getting in on this grand news.

Repent. "Repent" and "believe" are the two imperatives attached to Jesus' announcement. By "repent," perhaps Jesus had in mind covenant faithfulness (*covenant* simply meaning God's binding of himself to humanity and the mutual promises that agreement entails), the things people need to do in the new covenant to work cooperatively with God, the covenant-maker. First, he says repent. In Greek the word is *metanoia,* which means something like "think again" or "have a second thought" or scrutinize your whole way of doing life in light of what Jesus is saying. He wants us to assess our sense of vocation and determine whether we are living in God's story as his faithful partners.

Repentance is not merely related to salvation, as salvation is commonly misunderstood. It includes rethinking our religious profession, but it also includes a change of heart or determination to act differently in the whole of our life. This is crucial to being an obedient follower of Jesus. Repentance is an attitude and an ongoing lifestyle of humility and self-examination. It is not to be done in a morbid, self-deprecating way, but rather as a life-long journey of personal change through Jesus and his Spirit.

Believe. "Believe," here, has little to do with mental assent or intellectual effort. It has more to do with placing confidence in Jesus. It is a whole-life term. It means to act and live as if we actually trust that his announcement of the presence of the kingdom is true. Believing rightly, not in terms of mere content but by actually trusting Jesus, leads a Christ-follower to fulfill what it means to be in the "image of God." Here is an instructive thought from Eugene Peterson:

> Belief by its very nature requires assent and participation, trust and commitment. When we believe we are at our most personal and intimate . . . with the Other. Belief cannot be forced. If we are bullied or seduced or manipulated to believe, we do not end

up believing, we end up intimidated or raped or used. And we are less, not more.

Believe means something like "to trust in, rely on, and cling to" the kingdom announcement of Jesus. Belief is "obedient participation." In contrast, when we think of believing merely in the sense of mental assent to what Jesus says, our actual real life never comes into view. While the gospel certainly affects all issues related to our death and the afterlife, it first produces a new way of living, a new way of being God's people for the sake of others.

Belief refers to the active, implementing kind of trust pointed to in the parable of the wise and foolish builders at the end of the Sermon on the Mount:

> These words I speak to you are not incidental additions to your life, homeowner improvements to your standard of living. They are foundational words, words to build a life on. If you work these words into your life, you are like a smart carpenter. . . .
>
> But if you just use my words in Bible studies and don't work them into your life, you are like a stupid carpenter. (Matthew 7:24-26)

The kind of belief Jesus calls for shows up best in actions and attitudes, not merely in our brain. This kind of belief is not simply religious or having to do only with the incidentally religious aspect of life. It is the underpinning for all living, words to build a life on. They lead to the abundant life Jesus promised (John 10:10). *Belief* is the conviction, confidence and certainty that connects us to God's purpose in creating and relating to people—the creation covenant with the first humans (Genesis 1:26-30), the covenant with Abraham (Genesis 12:1-3), the covenantal renewal through Moses (Exodus 19–34), its fulfillment in Jesus, and the creation of the church at Pentecost (Luke 24:49, Acts 1:8; 2:4).

The kingdom of heaven is among us. The surprising gospel of Jesus creates a huge shift in thinking about what it means to be a Christian. Jesus' gospel invites us into an ongoing story. However, because of some misguided thinking, Christians often have a hard time finding their way into that story. I don't say this to produce guilt but as an invitation into the life God intends for us through the doorway of faith. In chapter three we'll find out how to unhook ourselves from the misguided thinking and free ourselves to live in Jesus' story.

A FREE AND SPACIOUS STORY

I like Johnny Cash, but I wasn't expecting a big theological breakthrough when my wife and I went to see the movie *Walk the Line*. I was surprised to find a significant nugget of truth—you never know where you'll find such things! A scene in the movie expresses well the theological and practical importance of telling the right story. Johnny Cash (J. R.) and his older brother, Jack, are lying in bed on a steamy summer night. To sum up a boyish argument Jack says, "Look J. R., if I'm gonna be a preacher some day, I'm gonna have to know the Bible front to back. You can't help nobody if you can't tell them the right story."

The right story isn't important because Peter will give us a pop quiz at the pearly gates. It is crucial because it provides the map for the journey, the canvas for the painting, the lyrics to sing, the lines to say in the drama. Story gives context. Proper context does wonderful things. It provides the motivation to learn. Retention rates soar because we now have a reason to learn and grow, to become an apprentice of Jesus in his story. Learning and growth happen when apprentices realize what they don't know, and why they need to know it. When we see the context, the big picture, we see how it applies to our life. Instead of just "going to heaven when I die," we now seek to fit our life into the story of what it means to be the cooperative friend of God.

This thought creates both freedom and focus: The Bible is a story, a grand, epic narrative. The scene is set, the plot, including the ending, is well-developed, but there is still some way to go, and we are invited to become living, participating, intelligent, and decision-making characters within the story as it moves toward its destination. Because nothing has more control over us than the story we think we are living in, this narrative has a central place in my life and teaching. Story is the most powerfully decisive organizing and shaping force in a person's life. It gives meaning to the various aspects of a life. Facts are good. Data is helpful. But they lose their power to explain or to motivate outside the context provided by story.

I believe the story of God and the story of Christianity have been so reduced that there is little of them for us to experience in this life. This is causing us—even sincerely religious people—to not live well. Many of us—as Jack feared—are caught in the grip of a wrong story. We are like the stereotypical lady held firmly in Godzilla's grasp, flailing away while Godzilla toys with her. To my knowledge there is no person, church, seminary or denomination to blame for this. Even if there were, finding blame is not what motivates me; helping others see the whole story is. Most likely you are reading this book because— whether a seeker, Christian leader or something in between—you too intuit that something is wrong with the American religious scene. You instinctually believe that we must move beyond mere belief and find a way to follow Jesus, a way that others around us experience as good.

When the story is lost or its plot lines mangled, the key facts normally associated with the Christian story—creation, sin, cross, resurrection, grace, forgiveness, heaven and hell—lose their proper meaning. For hundreds of years people studying the Bible have done so in fragmented ways. We've broken the text into its smallest parts— often individual words or portions of them—for analysis. Then we place them back into their sentence, paragraph, book, Testament and finally the whole Bible. It sounds reasonable, doesn't it? I'm not sure what went wrong here, but something did. In most cases the *story* was lost in this process. The smallest bits, when added up, never quite became a narrative again. In other cases the reassembled bits told a different, truncated story.

MEANING AND DIRECTION

Discovering the right story about God gives ultimate meaning and direction to life. Jesus, speaking to religious leaders of his day, says: "Do you have any idea how silly you look, writing a life's story that's wrong from start to finish, nitpicking over commas and semicolons?" (Matthew 23:24).

Here is the way I see this working: Perhaps you have heard the phrase "a storied sports franchise" (the Yankees or the Lakers), "a storied corporation" (IBM or Microsoft), "a storied orchestra" (the London Philharmonic) or "a storied dance troupe" (the Rockettes or the Bolshoi). *Storied* refers to something that has a celebrated, interesting, famous and important history. The "story" is preserved in these organizations through photos, clippings, archives, decorations and old-timers telling tales of yesteryear. These important and powerful symbols, icons and storytellers draw others into the story.

For instance, picture a young ballplayer as he walks into a famous locker room for the first time. As he does, he feels his very best effort being drawn out in light of the storied atmosphere. Similarly, a young executive, entering the board room where the business was built and the important decisions were made, feels inspired to fully apply her brightest ideas and most creative solutions to current challenges. She wants to live up to the successes of her predecessors.

Likewise, the gospel of the kingdom invites us into a large, all-encompassing story, the story that Adam and Eve, Israel, and the church were intended to dwell in. It is a huge privilege. In the Sermon on the Mount Jesus discussed all of the things humans pursue and how we worry about them. Then he said we must seek God's kingdom first and all these things will follow (Matthew 6:19-33). On the other hand there are serious ramifications for choosing to live outside God's story: a washed out life and wasted eternity.

Becoming a Christian is much like adopting a new life story. The biblical notion of repentance, of turning and going a new direction, is rightly viewed as choosing to say yes to God and his purposes. God's desire to interact with people involves our whole life, which means a change in thinking *and* much more. When we are converted, we switch stories, we reenter the plan of God. Like Michael Jordan deciding to stop playing minor-league baseball to play NBA basketball again, we do whatever it takes to fit our life into the new story. Our workout changes according to our new context: eat right, practice daily, do drills, get plenty of rest and so on.

Living into or embracing a new story, gaining a new sense of what life is all about, is what the biblical term *repentance* means. You may have heard that it means to "turn around and go in a different direction." It does mean that, but it means a whole lot more. It means something like seeing the call of God to humans, seeing his willingness to forgive us of our sins and to place us, by his power and grace at work in Jesus, back into his story. Then the only reasonable response is to rethink and realign every aspect of our life in light of this amazing opportunity. Repentance, properly understood, should become like gravity, pulling every area of our present and future life into the story of God. It is not just a reconsideration of our sinful past. Repentance includes all the activities and attitudes necessary to spiritual transformation into Christlikeness. It is the implementation process of switching stories.

When a single man with a career as a carpenter falls in love, gets married and feels called to become a high school teacher, he is, in a big way, switching the essential story lines of his life. He will have to rearrange all of his life to fit this new narrative. In response no one would say that going to college to get a teaching credential was some sort of overzealousness or fanaticism. And few would think that by pledging fidelity to the one he loves, he was being overly exclusive. We know that these are rational and normal things to do once he has made such a story-changing—"life changing"—decision.

A RATIONALE FOR CHRISTIAN PRACTICES

I have powerful childhood memories of trying to find ways to fulfill my dream of being a Major League Baseball player. I think these attempts parallel the activities associated with repentance—switching stories—and this kind of seeking can be truly childlike and godly. It does not have to neurotic, paranoid, religiously weird or legalistic. It has nothing to do with trying to earn something from God. I like the way one well-known radio personality puts it: "The great [religious] traditions are not systems for an impossible perfection but for aspiration to grace within the possibilities and the boundaries of every life, every moment." We may not be able to readily see it, but we can move into that kind of grace-filled life with a relaxed concentration, a peace that others experience as good.

Striving to please God is not a bad thing. Certainly Jesus' first followers were trying to do so (see Philippians 3). It pleases God to see his children arranging life's affairs to fulfill their God-given call or vision. This process feels like I am simply responding to something deep within me. It's a very natural thing to do.

I remember joyfully walking down Santa Ana's streets, passing under the rows of palm trees lining the library's sidewalk and through big glass doors. I would sit for hours reading books on how to hit a baseball. My favorite book at the time was by Ted Williams, the last player to hit over .400 for an entire season in the major leagues. Ted was "the" authority on hitting, especially when it came to being disciplined about the strike zone, about knowing which pitches to swing at and on what counts.

I realize now, with the benefit of forty years of hindsight, that the combination of regularly observing Williams (and other great hitters) and hearing his explanations of what he was attempting to do in the batter's box not only informed me, it transformed my imagination. I imagined standing like him at the plate, holding the bat the way he did, even trying to emulate his attitude, focus and confidence. Because I had a vision of being a major league hitter and decided to become one, I naturally sought out all types of means to become one, not just books on the subject.

When the vision of a different life—life in the kingdom—is clear and compelling, when we have firmly decided to follow it, we will certainly begin looking for means of implementation. I do this now in many ways in my attempt to follow Jesus, and for the most part I do it in a childlike manner. I've discovered that getting uptight about this stuff does no good. I've come to believe that Jesus actually knew what he was talking about when he said:

> What I'm trying to do here is to get you to relax, to not be so preoccupied with *getting*, so you can respond to God's *giving*. . . . Steep your life in God-reality, God-initiative, God-provisions. Don't worry about missing out. You'll find all your everyday human concerns will be met. Give your entire attention to what God is doing right now. (Matthew 6:31-34)

THE GREATEST OPPORTUNITY EVER GIVEN TO HUMANITY

For life change through changing stories to happen, we must give people a compelling reason to pursue spiritual transformation. We must help them see following Jesus in the kingdom as the greatest opportunity ever given to humanity. Jesus told the parables of the treasure buried in the field and the pearl of great price (see chap. 3) to help people clarify their attitudes about him and the eternal life he offered. Did they, like the pearl merchant and the real estate agent, see him and his agenda as valuable and desirable? A bargain so great that one would reasonably arrange all the affairs of their life to insure that they did not miss it? Where vision is strong and clear, it naturally pulls everything in a life into alignment with it.

Unfortunately, this is not clearly understood in our culture. Christianity is most often seen as having to do with forgiveness and heaven—not as a lifestyle of reorienting life to God's story as a Christ follower (see chap. 1). Lots of people say they believe in God—even in Jesus as Savior. But they have no intention of reordering life's affairs to effectuate that decision. They are like people who believe in flying but for whatever reason have no intention of ever boarding a plane, even when it is beneficial or necessary.

People who "believe" in God or Jesus but don't let them deeply penetrate their life never board the plane. The following words are John the Baptist's explanation of what was happening at the time of Jesus. It was a time in which the story of God was taking a dramatic turn. This turn became a revolution in the lives of those who got caught up in it:

> There at the Jordan River those who came to confess their sins were baptized into a *changed life*. . . . [John said,] "It's *your life that must change*. . . . What counts is your life. . . . I'm baptizing you here in the river, *turning your old life in for a kingdom life*. [Jesus]—will ignite the *kingdom life* within you, a fire within you, the Holy Spirit within you, changing you from the inside out." (Matthew 3:6, 8-9, 11, italics added)

Jesus' gospel is the greatest opportunity ever given humans because it involves their whole lives. *Life*—kingdom life—pops out all over the place in that passage. Not merely avoiding death or hell, but new life in Christ. When it comes to developing an imagination for Christian spirituality, the difference in emphasis is huge. The gospel gives me an imagination for living now, in the kingdom, not just a secure afterlife. It gives me hope for a changed life *now*, a Spirit-ignited life *now*, life in the kingdom *now*.

RESPONDING TO JESUS' GOSPEL

Because Jesus' gospel is all about life, my responsibility is to realign my life—with God's decisive help—to the unfolding redemptive story of Jesus and his kingdom. I am first a follower of Jesus, and, by the way, I am also married, a parent, a nurse, a teacher and the like.

Does the last sentence make you a little fearful that we could get too religious, go over-the-top with all this? I can see why. Maybe you are thinking of people you have known for whom religion messed up their lives. I too have struggled at times with an approach-avoidance syndrome regarding religion. But to be fair, we could also name amazing religious people who, organizing their lives around the sole vocation of following God in the way of Jesus, became just, generous and kind, and thus are wonderful mates, parents, workers, supervisors and students.

We tend to have a hard time imagining Jesus living in the twenty-first century—would he have an iPod, a Blackberry, a laptop? But let me see if I can give some new momentum to our spiritual lives by taking a look at Jesus' life. He had to struggle to make sense of his life and times. Sometimes we only see Jesus struggling in the garden before his crucifixion. But he was challenged daily to follow God in ways that were healing and freeing for the people he encountered.

Jesus had options for what it meant to be the faithful people of God. He could have chosen the quietist route and joined the separatist Qumran sect in their caves. But then how could he have been loving, teaching, healing and leading people? He might have selected the Herodian way of political compromise with the powers. But then how could he have disarmed them, tied them up and plundered their house? And he could have joined the Zealots, carrying a dagger and filling his heart with religiously inspired hate for Gentiles, Samaritans and errant Jews. But then how could he have been the kind of person who would never bend a reed, snuff out a smoldering wick or tell Peter to put away his sword?

It does not diminish Jesus' redemptive work on the cross to recognize that he is also the model and teacher for what it means to be servants of God. Jesus' *whole life* is our pattern. This is why many Christian leaders have written about him in terms of imitation. Imitation doesn't imply slavery. It doesn't mean we can't be ourselves or that we must try to live the life Jesus lived. It means we live the way he did: following the will of his Father. We follow the lead of the Holy Spirit in our daily life, using our personality, gifts and temperament. Jesus was humanity (Adam and Eve), Israel and the church as God intended them to be. We are like understudies, trying to act our part in life through the vision and values of Jesus' earlier part in the drama.

The prophets of Israel tried to help their people find their way into the story as well. They occasionally got out the script and read it to the people, admonishing them to find their place in the story. Jesus, through the conduct of his life, did the same. His life said, in effect, "The quietists, Zealots, Herodians, Pharisees, Sadducees and scribes have chosen the wrong stories! They are not living in covenant faithfulness with God. They have created and chosen their own ways. I am the way—watch how I do it! I have no agenda of my own. I work as my Father directs." Jesus' gospel (Mark 1:14-15), his attitude (Philippians 2:5-8), his cooperation with the story of God—even when difficult (John 5:17, 19, 20, 36; Hebrews 5:8), his explicit teachings ("Follow me") and his works (Luke 19:37; John 10:25, 32, 38) reveal the story, which adequately produces an imagination for spiritual transformation.

If the gospel is as Jesus explained—"The kingdom of God is near. Repent and believe the good news! . . . Come, follow me" (Mark 1:15, 17)—the big question is, What response does this evoke? Are you excited and joyful by this marvelous invitation to begin the adventure of following Jesus (which does, by the way, end in heaven)? Or does it sound oppressive because you don't want anyone messing with your present life, the story of your own making? In this context a seeker can intelligently decide for or against following Jesus and experiencing spiritual transformation—which is what it means to be a Christian.

JESUS' GOSPEL IS THE GIFT OF LIFE

I was once part of a work group that wrote a definition of *evangelism* under Dallas Willard's leadership. It helps us enter into the story of Jesus:

> Spiritual transformation into Christlikeness requires a conscious, clearheaded and public commitment to living as a disciple of Jesus Christ. That is, a decision to give our lives to him as his constant students, learning from him how to live all aspects of our lives as he would live them. Evangelism should be understood as a call to receive the gift of such a life.

Note the goal: spiritual transformation. Note also that it is active, not passive. No one wanders aimlessly into following Jesus. It is whole-life apprenticeship. It is a gift that God intends for all his creation.

Thus, being saved—being forgiven and placed back into good standing with God through the grace of Christ—may mean something like this:

> Through unmerited forgiveness I was spared the agony of missing the opportunity of living in the present rule and reign of God; rather, I found the pearl of great price and the treasure in the field.

Or:

> I was delivered from exile in the kingdom of self and transported to an eternal kind of life in which I know God and his Son (John 17:3), and I participate in what they are doing on the earth, which is the family business of the holy Trinity.

Or:

> I was healed of my mistrust of God. In Christ I now see how

utterly competent he is to be the guide for my life. I now can put my trust and confidence in Jesus (Matthew 7:24-25), which enables me, like a child, to take his hand and rely on him, to completely follow him into his kingdom, his story, learning to act and talk the way he did. And in so doing I now receive forgiveness and eternal life, the endless presence of God in the life to come, and avoid the eternal self-imposed trash heap of hell.

These comments are testimonies I have heard from friends who have grasped the new story. The comments are their way of explaining what happened to them when they reconsidered their whole life on the basis of Jesus' surprising gospel. For them, it led to a new kind of life. They came to see that according to Jesus' gospel, as John the Baptist said, it is our life that counts.

FOR REFLECTION AND DISCUSSION

1. Having heard Jesus' version (Mark 1:14-15, p. 34), how would you now explain the gospel to someone else?

2. What difference should it make now that you understand what *believe*—"to trust in, rely on, and cling to," "obedient participation"—means?

3. Similar to Jesus' situation, we have many ways of being a Christian. After reading this chapter, how will you decide what it means to be a Christian?

   What basis will you use for that choice?

4. Can you imagine repentance as a lifestyle? How might that work? How might it be received as a gift as Dallas Willard suggests?

IT'S OUR LIFE THAT COUNTS

Aligning with God's Story

The fear of flying is a clear and bright window into our difficulty of stepping into the story illuminated by Jesus' gospel. Because I travel a good deal, I often talk to people who tell me that they could never do what I do because they are afraid to fly. Imagine a conversation like this:

"What do you mean you're afraid to fly? Don't you believe in planes?" I ask my friend.

"Yes," Pete says, "I do believe in planes."

"Do you believe they fly?" I ask.

"Yes, I see them in the air almost every day," he responds.

"Do you acknowledge that planes rarely crash and that you are far more likely to get hurt in a car crash, hit by lightening or attacked by a shark than be in a plane accident?"

"Yes," my friend replies.

"Okay, then," I say. "Let's go to the airport."

Picture with me what happens next. Imagine Pete and me checking in at the counter, removing our shoes and taking all the metal from our pockets to pass through security, and walking together down the terminal to our gate. All seems to be going well. As our flight is called, we get out our tickets and approach the gate agent to give her our tickets. She shows us how to slide them through the machine at the gate, and we begin to walk down the jetway toward the door of the plane. As we approach the small gap between the jetway and the door of the plane, my friend refuses to cross the threshold. In that moment we look at each other and realize that my companion does not believe in flying. He gives mental assent to it, but he cannot place his confidence in it.

BELIEF HAS TO DO WITH CONFIDENCE IN JESUS

That small one- or two-inch gap between the jetway and the aircraft door is the exact place many people refuse to follow Jesus into his kind of life.

I need to quickly point out that I am not saying that *knowledge* is utterly unimportant. Knowing is important, but it's not the whole deal, as it's often made out to be. We need knowledge that helps us "live tomorrow" in the realm of God—the kingdom—that is here.

Let me suggest what I think is the best explanation for why knowledge is important. To act or behave well, we must think straight enough to participate within the rules of the game or, in the case of Christianity, to act within the biblical story. Otherwise, it would be like trying to play football with the rules of soccer. This wouldn't work, no matter how sincerely the beliefs were held. We simply can't follow Jesus through the "rules" of an errant version of Christianity or through the tenets of another religion or through a nonreligious worldview.

Permit me a golf illustration—but any behavioral or action-based example would do. You and I are having lunch in a restaurant when Tiger Woods and Annika Sörenstam walk in. I say, "Look, here come two people who really know golf." Would you think I mean that they know the history of golf? Would you think I mean they know the rules of golf? Wouldn't you immediately know that I mean to say that they know how to play golf? Playing is a whole-person, practiced reality.

While Annika and Tiger do know the rules and history of their game, that mental knowledge alone is not what allows them to play golf, to be the best golfers in the world. No, their knowledge is connected to years of doing what it takes to live their dream.

No Story or the Wrong Story

Lots of Christians are stuck knowing something of the history and rules of Christianity, but it does not translate into a different kind of life. There is also a growing group of people with a different challenge: they know little to nothing of the Christian story. Whether no story or the wrong story, each prevents us from pulling our life into alignment with God—and it really is our life that counts. This pursuit of God and his story has nothing to do with earning some advantage from God, avoiding hell or achieving heaven; it is born from simple, focused desire to arrange our life to follow Jesus. Annika and Tiger arranged their lives to fit into the story of golf. We face the exact same process, just with a different outcome in mind.

Trust me, God is not somehow offended by our desire to work alongside him. Such actions should not be misconstrued as "works righteousness," that is, earning salvation from God. Thinking about it this way might help: God did not, after creating Adam and Eve, say, "Now go and merely relate. Just have community with each other and with me." Sometimes we think of work and its associated intentionality as a part of the curse. But it is not so. God actually said to Adam and Eve, "Come, work with me. Be my co-laborers, my subcontractors, in this cool new creation I have just started. It will be utterly satisfying to you—it is what you are made for. And by the way, in the process of doing stuff together you, the human community, and I will develop genuine, nonutilitarian relationships. Instead of feeling used, you will feel like a devoted dancer who finally got to Carnegie Hall with all her best friends" (my paraphrase of Genesis 2).

Of course the Fall into sin and the resulting curse changed everything. Cooperating with God's intended story for humans must be intentional on our part. This is especially true now that, after the first sin, we know more than good: We know evil and how to use it. We know power and authority and how to abuse them. This is why intentional spiritual transformation is so important: it's only in this way that we can become the kind of people God dreamed of.

Jesus told two parables to help potential followers clarify in their minds their intention to follow him. It seems Jesus wanted to help us understand what it would take—our inner motivation and the engagement of our will (in cooperation with God's initiation)—to follow him. The two parables are about a hidden treasure buried in a field, and a pearl of great value. Once we knew of the treasure or the pearl, in order to get either of them we would have to reorganize aspects of our life—such as selling property or other possessions—to purchase the land with the hidden treasure or to buy the prized pearl (Matthew 13:44-45).

This is a place where sincere Christians often get confused. They are afraid that the cooperation alluded to—selling one thing to get something else, doing due diligence, placing "For Sale" ads or phoning brokers—when applied to religion will lead to human pride, legalism, works righteousness or the devaluing of the sacrifice of Christ on the cross.

But Jesus was not confused. He was simply being practical. He was saying something like, "If you really want to live in the kingdom of God, if you desire a life derived from and lived in the kingdom, you'll have to arrange your daily affairs to do so." A similar theme is in view when Jesus says, "Anyone who won't shoulder his own cross and follow behind me can't be my disciple" (Luke 14:27). Jesus is not ranting like a ticked-off parent who might say to her child, "Unless you clean your room you cannot go to the movies!" Jesus is not saying that unless you live a life of self-sacrifice he will not let you be his follower. He is simply saying you can't have it both ways—

it's simply impossible to follow him while trying to have your own agenda. Jesus is saying something like "unless you fill your car with gas you can't follow me from Reno to Los Angeles." It's a simple, no-nonsense statement of fact.

ONE VOCATION

If it is our life that counts, it may do us well to stop for a moment and reconsider the meaning of the word *vocation*. I'll bet most of us associate vocation with our career, our job or what we get paid to do. This is especially true if we think our job matches our skills well and makes us content. Then we might say so-and-so "has found his vocation" or "her calling." It is true that the Latin word for "calling" can mean to hear a voice, a summons or strong inclination to a particular state or course of action, the special function of a person or a group, the work in which a person is regularly employed.

We have kept in our common language the latter, functional, usage but have lost the part concerning hearing a call from another. *Summons*, *calling* and *hearing a voice* all suggest personal interaction. Calling is like the phone game many of us played as kids, with two tin cans tied to ends of a string. What we heard was not impersonal but the person on the other end of the string. Likewise, vocation or calling is about much more than what we *do*. It is one person—God—calling to another person—me.

Cooperating with God, growing in him for the sake of others, is our singular vocation, no matter what we do to get a paycheck. We are principally called to God and his purposes. Fix this in your imagination—following Jesus is our special function—and the rest will fall into place. It becomes our self-conscious identity. We can live this vision out as school teachers, police officers, business partners, actors, managers or construction workers. Life suddenly pops with meaning, power and adventure.

This—cooperating with God—is why we were created. We all

seek it instinctively. Some of us have sought it in the wrong places and by wrong means, hurting ourselves and others along the way. But it is not too late. Our story, as seen in the pages of the Bible and in the narratives of church history, reveals how God rescues people from Houdini-like traps, giving freedom, granting fresh starts and empowering new beginnings.

PRACTICES FOR A LIFE THAT COUNTS

Spring 1999 came to me not merely as the routine cycle of seasons—shoveling snow, planting tulips, mowing the lawn and raking leaves. My friend and mentor, John Wimber, had recently died, leaving me to supervise the five-hundred-plus Vineyard churches in America, to insure that they stayed together and kept the path laid out by their founder. I was also personally distracted. No, it was more than that: my wife and I were in the grip of a monster called breast cancer. To top it off, there was the mad build-up to Y2K.

But, as often happens in life, Y2K was only the tip of my iceberg of trials and challenges. It really got personal during what was otherwise a once-in-a-lifetime kind of trip to Switzerland. Along with friends and colleagues, my wife and I were enjoying each other as well as the chalet, the view of the slopes and, most spectacularly, the helicopter ride to the summit of the Matterhorn in Zermat.

The free fall began the next morning when, while I was shaving in a brightly lit bathroom, my wife noticed a peculiar mole on my back. She thought it looked suspicious and demanded that I get it checked as soon as I got home. There was one big problem for me: the national Vineyard pastor's conference was coming up. It was the first one since our founder's death—a kind of coming out party for me—one of those moments where you are expected to be, and want to be, at your best. I had no time for doctors; the conference was only a couple of weeks away.

But cancer had already visited our home, and my wife knew how

dangerous it was. She insisted that I get the mole examined. I gave in
and went to the dermatologist. I waited for a few minutes by myself in
the cramped but orderly room. Soon the door swung open and I heard
the words "Take your shirt off, young man. Let's have a look at that
thing." The doctor took a quick look and said, "I've been at this a long
time, and I can tell you that you almost certainly have melanoma."

To make sure his naked-eye diagnosis was accurate, a nurse led
me down a short hall to a room where the doctor took out a chunk
of flesh. The tissue was sent to the best specialist my doctor knew.
Confirmation came back: melanoma indeed. Surgery was scheduled
with the melanoma specialists at the UCLA Medical Center in Los
Angeles.

"Sorry," I announced to anyone who would listen, "I do not have
time for a surgery, I have a conference to run and at which I must give
the main talks."

"Okay," the doctor said, "a couple weeks won't make a big difference, but you get in here the day the conference is over."

"Deal!" I said.

During our conference, I attended a workshop led by Richard Foster, a friend I admire and trust when it comes to guidance into "the
real and lasting life." The workshop title was "An Introduction to the
Spiritual Disciplines," a practical and useful overview of the disciplines
most practiced by Christians throughout our two-thousand-year history. The one Richard listed last—and, running out of time, all he
could do was say a sentence about it—was the discipline of *submission*. I had never heard of this discipline and was intrigued. Richard
described it as "routinely choosing to not have your own way, to seek
opportunities to not be in control, preferably in ways that are hidden
to, and good for others." That definition stuck. Being a perfectionist,
one who tries to control all aspects of life, I realized that submission
was something I would need to work on if I was going to follow Jesus.
Little did I know that my first opportunity to employ this new disci-

pline would occur during one of the most uncomfortable and over-whelming moments of my life.

Richard's talk still echoed in my mind as the conference ended. The conference had been a success. All my self-focused fears proved unfounded. Then came the dreaded day after the conference, the one on which I had agreed to have the cancer surgery at UCLA. Here's an important part of the story: All of the stress I was experiencing during this time was leading to occasional mild panic attacks expressed in claustrophobia. I was increasingly uncomfortable in small, closed-in spaces like elevators, small rooms and airplanes.

On this particular hot Southern California day, I began to feel claustrophobic as we pulled the car into the muggy underground garage at UCLA. *Okay*, I thought to myself, *I can deal with this. Please just let the elevator not be full. Great*, I sarcastically said to myself as the elevator doors opened. It was lunch hour and the elevator was full of white-garbed medical people, causing the panic to increase palpably.

I was put into a very small, nondescript room and told to disrobe. Naked, except for the hospital gown, I was about as uncomfortable as a human being could be. You know—you wish somehow your inner itch could be scratched but there is just no way. There was no way out for me.

Just as I was wondering if someone could die of panic, Richard Foster's words on the spiritual discipline of submission rushed into my consciousness: "routinely choosing to not have your own way, to seek opportunities to not be in control, . . . to be mindful that one is always safe in the kingdom of God."

This may sound too good to be true, but, with God as my witness, as those thoughts passed through my psyche, I could feel my whole physiology change. My nerves calmed, my temperature cooled and my brain returned to tranquil mode. In short, my inner-person seemed to be reworked—at least for that moment. I found out later that it works most of the time. But the disciplines are not tricks or tools you pull out of a bag to get through an uncomfortable circumstance. Rather, they are practices to employ during the daily events of our lives—like I did that day in the hospital. As we routinely do this, we are rewired by the power and grace of God; we are permanently changed into the image of Jesus.

CAUTION: YOU MAY BE TEMPTED TO ENTER THE "NO" ZONE

While I need the discipline of submission, not to mention other disciplines, to live a life that counts, there is a very important caution for the journey ahead, a trap to avoid, which many of our most sincere predecessors in the faith have fallen into. This new life is not a series of *nos* or *don't do thats.*

I'm not talking about quitting illegal drugs, or stopping the relentless pursuit of sex or money or power, or refusing to lie or steal, and the like. Of course, all of these are out of alignment with being the cooperative friends of God. They cause untold human suffering. They are sins. They miss the mark of God's intention for his people, and are therefore to be overcome in the journey of spiritual transformation into Christlikeness. It can be done—just not in a *no* oriented way. They are best overcome in a *yes* oriented way—yes to God and yes to others.

Though it won't appear in the newspapers like the big sins committed by famous Christian leaders, normal people like you and me actually do find a new and different life in Jesus. Paul tells us how to move along in life with Jesus: "Everything—and I do mean everything—connected with that old way of life has to go. It's rotten through and through. Get rid of it! And then take on an entirely new way of life—a God-fashioned life, a life renewed from the inside and working itself into your conduct as God accurately reproduces his character in you" (Ephesians 4:22-24). Though there is stuff that has to go, the focus is on "a life renewed."

The history of the church abounds with examples of disciples of

Jesus who followed him into this kind of life, through the presence, power and guidance of the Holy Spirit. Scripture is true: "God brings the best out of you, develops well-formed maturity in you" (Romans 12:2). God is not a tyrant in this story. What he "gets" from you—and what others get from you in your service to them—is ultimately for your good. Trust me; you'll experience this kind of life as the best thing that ever happened to you. You'll experience a feeling of purpose that you've never known. You'll become fully human, fully alive, humanity as God intended.

ALIGNMENT WITH GOD'S STORY

Eugene Peterson's use of the word *align* in *The Message* helps me envision what it means to be a Christian, what it means that "our life counts." It helps me connect Jesus' gospel to my life. In the Gospel of John Jesus says:

> It's urgent that you listen carefully to this: Anyone here who believes what I am saying right now and aligns himself with the Father, who has in fact put me in charge, has at this very moment the real, lasting life and is no longer condemned to be an outsider. This person has taken a giant step from the world of the dead to the world of the living. (John 5:24)

In this passage, it seems that Jesus' guiding thought is one of unity or continuity. He roots his words in "the Father." His invitation to align our life with his is connected to his alignment with the Father. Jesus' dream for his followers is that in this three-way alignment— Father-Son-Christians—they would find life, the real and lasting life, the new life that begins with faith and never ends in world to come.

With an ever-increasing effectiveness contemporary society produces disconnected and lonely people. One of the greatest healings associated with new life in Jesus is that we are no longer disconnected, no longer outside of God, no longer at the fringe of humanity. Our linkage with God and humanity is right at the heart of what it means to be a Christian. As you'll see in the coming chapters, experiencing this double-connected reality is critical to being Jesus' cooperative friends for the sake of others.

A comment on "the world of the dead" in the John 5 passage: This doesn't mean the nether world. The world of the dead is all around us. Any campus, workplace or neighborhood reveals faces of the walking dead—those not cooperating with God. Jesus says there is a way out of this world: alignment with the Father through the Son. The world of the living is not a place either. It too is all around us, inhabited by those who are aligning their lives with the good news of Jesus, the gospel of the kingdom.

Let's look at the benefits of aligning with Jesus. Jesus says, "I am the Bread of Life. The person who aligns with me hungers no more and thirsts no more, ever" (John 6:35). Here Peterson translates *believes in* as "aligns with." This, I believe, is significant evangelistically because it focuses on life, and pastorally because it provides grounds for spiritual formation. *Align* highlights the synergism of the two components of faith: belief and behavior. Faith leads to life, to the source of life, to Jesus who is the Bread of Life. Life in Jesus satisfies all the deepest human longings—especially spiritual ones. Speaking spiritually, those with quenched thirst and filled bellies are free to give to others water and food, that is, love and healing, acceptance and respect. This principle of being "full in order to fill others" is at the heart of a new way to live (see part 2 of this book).

In the same John passage, Jesus also says, "This is what my Father wants: that anyone who sees the Son and trusts who he is and what he does and then aligns with him will enter real life, eternal life" (John 6:40). Those who see the Son and trust him recognize who he is and what he is up to; they discern the work of God in Jesus and thus place their trust in him. Here *trust* means to place one's confidence, dependence and hope in Jesus. Without trust it is impossible to align

our life with Jesus. Alignment presupposes a straight, correct or authoritative reality to which something else is adjusted. For us, getting
straight with that reality requires that we believe something good,
something better than what we are now experiencing, will happen
when we align ourself to it. Jesus said that was exactly the case. The
person who sees, trusts and aligns him- or herself with Jesus is given
a new kind of life.

Alignment means falling into a set (story) line, being in the correct
position relative to the (plot) line. This is a great way to understand
the repentance called for by the prophets, John the Baptist, Jesus and
the New Testament writers. Alignment through repentance is simple
cooperation with the story of God, which is a good definition of what
it means to be a Christian. Of secondary importance is the fact that it
also avoids God's wrath. But our motive is positive embodiment, not
negative avoidance. I want to align my life with things that generate
respect, gratitude and awe, not fear.

FROM THE INSIDE OUT

That day in the hospital, the moment I felt my physiology change,
taught me something. The new kind of life, which comes when we are
aligned with God's plan and live for the sake of others, comes from the
inside out. Something changed *in* me—then in peace I could deal with
reality around me. We cannot wish or hope ourself into this kind of
life. We cannot simply will ourself into it either. This life is initiated
and sustained by God, and practiced by Jesus' followers, who practice
disciplines, like submission.

None of us seek alignment with God as a blank slate or white-
board. I started moving toward God as an already spiritually formed
person—in both positive and negative ways. Some of me works well
with a life of alignment to God, while other aspects, judging by my
actual behavior, scream no! Thus some of my previous misalignment
makes it difficult for me to embody a life rooted in the story of be-

ing the cooperative friend of God for the sake of others. When I see profound weakness, sickness and intense poverty, I get scared. It's not that I don't care about these realities; they overwhelm me. They leave me feeling out of my depth—out of control.

Thus I need to be spiritually transformed in order to align myself with God's story, to be a filled person who can subsequently serve those in need. I'm sure raging fire and horrible injury are not pleasant, but the firefighters rush in anyway. It's my sense that God created humanity for and, more precisely, called Israel and Christians to such a life of "rushing in." And such a life is a gift. We don't pursue this kind of life to get God to like us. Being humanity as God intended is a pure gift of God's love and grace. It is the greatest privilege ever offered to humans.

Understanding the story of God—"Oh, I get it now, the firefighters of God rush in"—has a transforming effect on our mind. We no longer "conform . . . to the pattern of this world" (Romans 12:2 NIV). We do this by aligning our life to a new pattern. Or we no longer live in the old story. Rather, we live in the new story of the kingdom, the cooperative people of God. The key is not the old that is left behind— though that is a necessary first step. The real power is in the new story. This is where God lives, moves and has his being. There, we are made whole, restored and reconciled. As we begin to embody the new story in the events and interactions of our life, we are transformed, changed from the inside out. (See appendix 3 for a scriptural overview of life.)

NEW LIFE GROWS BEST WITHIN A COMMUNITY OF FAITH

In chapter four I will explain how communities of faith, churches, work with us in our spiritual transformation. I realize that many people are turned off by church. As I travel, I overhear the talk. (You should hear how some people respond when I tell them what I do for a living.) I read most the studies on the attitudes of outsiders to the church. Nevertheless, the church is critically important to following Jesus.

The people of God have never been perfect. Adam and Eve weren't. Neither were Abraham, Israel, the disciples of Jesus or the early Christians. But even though this truth is frustrating, there is no other place to run, no place to hide. The church is, after all, God's chosen means to express himself on earth.

Yes, there is a great deal of angst about church today; its reputation is in decline. But the church is like the stock market; it may go down for a while but over time it rebounds. And the reality is that the church is important for those of us who are growing, struggling and seeking transformation.

FOR REFLECTION AND DISCUSSION

1. Like a person who "believes" in flying but is afraid to board the plane, have you experienced notional faith (mere mental assent) versus practical faith (confident action)? If so, how did you move from the one to the other?

2. In a few sentences, explain the story you have been living.

3. Explain what alignment means. Did this concept help you understand the process of switching stories?

4. Do you see the value in realigning your life to God's story? Why or why not?

THE ROLE OF THE CHURCH

Jesus Is Not Just Your Personal Savior

"I am not sure I trust you." Those are not the words a church planter/ pastor wants to hear. In fact, I don't think I *heard* them, but I remember *feeling* them somewhere deep in my belly. Jan (not her real name) was a new assistant in my office. At the time I was working for a nonprofit foundation. We were coaching church planters in various denominations all over the world. Jan had been an acquaintance at church, but I didn't really know her until she started coming to our home for our new church plant's core group meetings. From Jan and her friends I started learning how much they distrusted church and Christian leaders. The church seemed unsafe to them. They experienced it as fickle and hypocritical.

Thus, I was surprised when Jan agreed to work with me in a religious nonprofit. She was bright, hard-working and easy to be around. Having noticed those traits, one day as we were discussing the difficulty many in her generation were having with church, I asked Jan, "Why do you trust us?" That's when I heard—felt—the gut-wrenching words.

In the months and years that followed we learned a great deal about ourselves and the role of church in the world. Thankfully, we came to the place where we were willing to hazard being a community of faith—complete with all of the associated risks and rewards.

MORE THAN A PERSONAL SAVIOR

Is Jesus your personal Savior? We've asked and been asked that question so many times that it has reduced Jesus to just that: a *personal* Savior. I know why we asked that question so many times over the last few decades. We wanted to make sure that no one was merely a cultural, denominational or family-of-origin Christian. But this inadvertently reduced Jesus to the size of a human heart—the place we were supposed to invite this "personal" Savior. This is not a great fit for the King, whose kingdom encompasses the cosmos and transcends space and time. Learning from the surprising gospel of Jesus that "my" life counts only gets me part of the way along the journey. Salvation is necessarily personal, but it is not merely personal.

We are saved into a people and into a story. This is why the New Testament is so unrelenting in its vision and demand for one new people—a people who existed first for God and second for others. I know this may sound a little strange on first hearing because we are used to thinking about forgiveness and heaven as the core of what it means to be a Christian. Hang on to those two things, but set alongside them this: living as the people of God for the sake of others.

To reimagine what it means to be a Christian we must move beyond the notion that Jesus is *only* a personal Savior. We cannot be the cooperative friends of Jesus who creatively seek to be good for the sake of others, if we see Christianity as essentially personal. It *is* personal—but within an overall context of a people with a purpose.

It takes a people to do what the church is called to do. Otherwise the transformed life is too overwhelming, even depressing, if we are sensitive to what is going on around us. Some days I feel the need to remove every news link on my computer: hundreds dead in an attack; thousands dead in a natural disaster; families' homes destroyed in a tornado; murders; deaths from disease; marital breakups; and sins of well-known clergy. It never ends.

The other day I visited a family friend in a hospital's intensive care/

oncology unit. Our daughter babysits the family's kids when the parents go out. The eleven-year-old boy has a very serious form of leukemia. When we walked into the room, he was obviously very sick and very uncomfortable.

Though I've been a pastor for decades, I still have a terrible time in hospitals. I feel peoples' pain. I get slightly sick to my stomach and feel strange sensations from my upper legs to my chest. Weird, I know. We moved outside the room to give the boy and his family some privacy. While standing there, someone pointed out a young woman sitting in the nurse's station looking at a computer screen. I assumed it was a hospital worker until I was told she had just lost her husband and two children in a bizarre car crash and that her remaining child, who was also in the car, was in critical condition. Situations like this are crushing. They make us feel impotent, powerless. No matter where I turned my head there was tragedy: a devastated wife and mother here, our young friend with leukemia there, and a TV blaring the latest mishap in the waiting room.

All this can become mind numbing and, worse, heart-and-soul deadening. If we're not careful, it can shut us down. We need to see that *I* am not responsible to remedy all this, but as *we* respond together as God's people true healing will be found.

In the new way of Jesus, in the life of the kingdom, social division and partiality must be removed. This is crucial because becoming a Christian, growing as a Christian and serving others, is not a solo enterprise. It happens in the community of faith. There are no rugged individuals in the church. In God's renewed humanity we see that all persons—regardless of gender, race, ability or nationality—have parts to play in his story.

Without community, without our fellow actors in the story, we have no one to interact with, no one to speak our lines to, and no one to respond to us. Just as it takes a village to raise a child, it takes a community of faith to shape and enable an individual on the journey of faith. God is not saving individuals alone. He is creating a people for himself as his cooperative friends. And only among this *people* do we derive a genuine sense of *person*.

COMMUNITIES TRAINED TO RESPOND

I am amazed by the men and women who are society's first responders to disasters or crisis situations. They don't stop to think; they instinctively do what has been drilled into them through repeated practice. They don't panic or fold (unlike me in a hospital setting). Whenever I see them in action, I think, *Wow, they are really living in their story; they are faithfully acting their part.* When a crisis is announced, when things are far from routine, the first responders begin their routines, what they are trained to do through years of inner and outward disciplines. They respond for the sake of others, practicing their disciplines in the worst situations our world has to offer. They are models for how the ambassadors of the kingdom of God should respond to the world.

I think God envisions something like that for the church. N. T. Wright helpfully puts the matter like this: "God's covenant purpose was to choose a people in and through whom the world would be healed. That purpose, reaching its climax in the Messiah, is now to be worked out through his people." I resonate with this statement of the purpose of God's people. But it leaves us dangling. One large detail is missing: Who are God's people? What exactly is the church?

The church is not a *place* you go to; it is a community, a group you participate in. Now, I don't mean to criticize the local church's leaders or its weekend services and programs, but church meetings are not "the game." They prepare us for the game. If the church is a people, and this is what Scripture teaches, we can be likened to a basketball team, a dance troupe or a musical group. All teams meet—as Christians do for worship, Bible studies, prayer meetings and fellowship. But basketball, dance and music teams know one vital thing that the church often forgets: teams meet to prepare to play the game. Meetings are not the game. Christianity—following Jesus—is not lived, is not fully expressed, within the walls of the church building but in the routines of daily life.

Our current, real lives—no matter what they are—are the place we practice our spirituality, where we are the church. We don't need to add a bunch of religious stuff to an already full life in order to be the church or to please God. Jesus served God as a carpenter and lived an abundant life of joy. Jesus could very easily have had your job or role in life. (This is true whether you work in a position usually occupied by males or females.) Even in your specific work or position in life, Jesus could have lived his life of obedience. *Okay,* you may be thinking, *I get your point. But how does "church" fit into my life of following Jesus and serving others in my daily routines?*

WHAT IS THE CHURCH?

A couple of kindergarten-level drawings may help us finally get an unforgettable image of the church in your minds. Take a moment to imagine yourself sketching a picture of the church on a restaurant napkin. What did you picture? I'll bet it was a square or rectangle with a pointed roof line, topped by a cross. Right? It would be so much better to draw a bunch of stick-figure people doing life and mission together. I'm not down on buildings; I'm up on the people of God. I want to make them the center of our image of the church.

Working against the image of the church as a sent people are three common misconceptions. The vast majority of Americans would define the church in one of three ways: church as a place ("I go the Crystal Cathedral"), an event ("I went to Mass today") or a famous pastor ("I go to Rick Warren's church"). Hoping to change these wrong ideas without casting local churches aside as irrelevant relics, I offer a definition of *church* that puts it in its proper, penultimate place: The church is created and governed by the calling and sending activity of God.

The church is secondary to the kingdom of God in that it is the instrument or means through which God regularly expresses himself.

As long as local churches see themselves in this light and conduct their activities for the purpose of equipping and releasing God's people to follow Jesus and serve others during the 167 hours of a week they are not in church, they are doing fine and need not be criticized. They have a legitimate, God-given role to play. These "team meetings" can be designed to help people perform better as followers and servants in the real game being played outside of the church building.

Any church can do this. It is not necessary to have a big building, a big budget or a well-known pastor. All it takes is hearing the new story and deciding to organize around it. That decision is, of course, an act of leadership. In my many years in church work, I've never known someone so incompetent that they couldn't make a decision like that. They may not have the gifts of persuasion to win the argument, but that's okay. Even biblical leaders—including Jesus—heard the people say, "No way. We're not following you into that story!"

A COMMUNITY THAT SUPPORTS DAILY LIFE

Unlike some, I see hope for local churches. There is nothing wrong with them that can't be fixed by agreeing to travel together on the inward and outward journeys. Churches don't need newer or larger buildings to do this. Nor do they need more staff, parking or nursery space. What they need is a clear vision to be the sent people of God. Once that vision is agreed to, all that's left to do is to organize the budget, calendar and meetings around embodying that vision. No one will get it perfect. There will be slip-ups and miscalculations. But as the story of the people of God in Bible tells us, this is all a part of the process.

Here is a final thought: All we'll take with us into eternity is the kind of people we become on our journey. No building will go; no event is eternal. So don't worry about getting "church" just right. Focus on faithfulness and alignment with the intention of God. These will last. Churches that prepare followers of Jesus for the kingdom, which is eternal, have got it right: "They will rule with [the Master] age after age after age" (Revelation 22:5).

Much of the church has participated in the wrong story: that Christ is merely our "personal" Savior, and salvation is going to heaven when we die. This story does not fire up our imagination for this life; it gives no coherent purpose for the community of faith or its activities; and it provides a faulty view of the life to come. But when we catch the true vision of the church and align ourselves with God's kingdom in Christ, most of the present consumerist bickering and quibbling about church life will simply drift away.

Church is a community of people created by the kingdom of God, which is the expressed intent of God, his rule and reign. Local churches—gatherings of Christ's followers—exist as outposts of God's kingdom agenda. It's really that simple. And the devil is not in the details. The devil is in the wrong story, which produces a wrong mental picture and wrong pattern for church life. Now we know better. Let's form new churches and reform existing ones that naturally and routinely embody God's story. Such churches are the soil out of which grow cooperative friends of Jesus.

If Christians adopted their everyday spheres of influence as the place to embody, announce and demonstrate the gospel of the kingdom, I can imagine several nurses on the same shift serving Christ on their floor, families living in the same apartment complex ministering to their neighbors, and police officers banding together to reach out to the community. I foresee little bands of Christ-followers agreeing to go on the "inner journey and outer journey" together. Those who journey inward together seek spiritual transformation into Christlikeness. On the outward journey they seek to become the kind of people from whom deeds of goodness in service to others naturally flow.

This double journey is very self-consciously done for the sake of others, not for personal piety or to earn anything from God or to impress others. The focus of the dual journey is fitting ourselves for life in the kingdom, empowered by the Holy Spirit for the sake of others. In the midst of this new life we come together weekly to worship God with others. But this doesn't mean that our 167 hours outside of the church building isn't worship. Whenever I am tempted to think that way I reread Romans 12:1, which says, "Take your everyday, ordinary life—your sleeping, eating, going-to-work and walking-around life—and place it before God as an offering." These activities can be worship as much as singing songs, reciting the liturgy, reading Scripture or saying a prayer.

SUMMARIZING MY VIEW OF THE CHURCH

This chapter is not a full-blown theology of the church. I have endeavored to say only two simple but crucial things about the church: (1) Though it is not perfect, and I understand why people are skeptical of it, there is hope for the church. (2) For followers of Jesus there is nowhere else to go. The church is God's chosen vessel. We need to be with God's people in order to grow, and the scope of the work—healing the world in partnership with God—demands that we join the church in its healing efforts.

In the second part of this book I will give you a straightforward, easily passed-on vision for a new kind of life rooted in our new understanding of what it means to be a Christian. I will lay out my dream for being cooperative friends of Jesus, living consistent lives of creative goodness for the sake of others through the power of the Holy Spirit.

FOR REFLECTION AND DISCUSSION

1. Define what the church is in your own words.

2. In this chapter the church is pictured two ways: as a building and as stick-figure people. When you were asked to imagine sketching the

church on a restaurant napkin, which one came to your mind first? Why?

3. When we think "church," we tend to think of it in terms of group gatherings or meetings. Does thinking of the church in its scattered state, as people dispersed in their daily endeavors, give you new ways of imagining being the cooperative friends of Jesus?

PART TWO

A New Way to Live

COOPERATIVE FRIENDS OF JESUS

Maybe Jesus Didn't Intend to
Start a World Religion

We neither make nor save ourselves.

God does both the making and saving.

He creates each of us by Christ Jesus to join him in the work he does,

the good work he has gotten ready for us to do,

work we had better be doing.

EPHESIANS 2:10

"So what?" the pragmatist asks.

I've made some significant assertions thus far. I've said that we are confused about the very thing Jesus came to bring—eternal life. I've suggested that the Christian story is often misunderstood, reduced to a story about going to heaven upon death. Thus the story incorrectly centers on forgiveness of sins without locating forgiveness in its larger narrative. I've been setting forth a new way of thinking, which is actually the original story, about what it means to be a Christian. The story centers on the notion of being the people of God, with heaven as the destination and spiritual formation as the goal. The wrong telling starts the story at the Fall (Genesis 3), missing God's ultimate intention of having cooperative friends who seek to live in creative goodness for the sake of others through the power of the Holy Spirit (Genesis 1–2).

If you haven't noticed, I have been repeatedly using four phrases to capsulize the story of the Christian life. God intends for the followers of Jesus to be his (1) cooperative friends (2) seeking to live in creative goodness (3) for the sake of others (4) through the power of the Holy Spirit. In this chapter I will unpack the first of those four phrases. I aim to put some meat on answering the question, What would I do if I knew I was going to live tomorrow? In this and the following three chapters I'll spell out the answers I find helpful. This is the basis on which I organize my life. I commend it to you as well.

A friend of mine, along with a couple of her friends, has been trying to live this way for a few years. Here is one small example of how they try to be cooperative friends:

> Easter was approaching and everywhere I looked it seemed to be all about the bunny. I started thinking about what I could do to put Jesus back front and center. I remembered attending a Passover Seder dinner at a local church some years before. It had been led by a pastor who has both a Jewish and Christian background. I remembered being fascinated by many of the things he shared about the ceremony and how it foretold Jesus' sacrifice. I researched the traditional Passover celebration and began to imagine what it would have been like to be there with Jesus.
>
> I called one of my friends in my small group and talked with her about putting together a Seder dinner but adding to the ceremony what we know from the Gospels about what Jesus said

and did. The Holy Spirit must have been working with her too, because she bubbled over with ideas and thoughts about how we could proceed. My son built some low tables so we could "recline" on pillows on the floor and moved the furniture out of the living room so we could squeeze fifteen people in. My friend put together a fabulous menu using food typical for Jerusalem around the time of the Last Supper. Friends and family helped set up and serve. I printed up a Messianic Haggadah to give to all the guests so they could participate in the reading.

Over the past few years, we have put on eight Last Supper dinners with approximately 25 percent of the guests being unchurched (who, by the way, were the most enthusiastic about the experience!). It is a great way to invite your unchurched friends to come and experience Jesus. All in all, the most incredible and wondrous thing about doing this is how the Holy Spirit took control and filled us all with such energy and joy. What would have normally felt like work was in fact one of the most fun activities I have ever done (way better even than winning the Newport/Ensenada regatta!).

I use the image of cooperative friends because it reflects God's ultimate intention. It does a great job of locating the Christian life in God's story. Eugene Peterson gives me a vision for a more full-orbed, all-embracing Christianity:

> The text for Christian living, . . . set within the spacious contours of this Jesus-welcoming, Spirit-anchored, God-defined, and Trinity-framed context, is the Bible, our Holy Scriptures. This Bible turns out to be a large, comprehensive story, a *metastory*. The Christian life is conducted in story conditions. The Bible is basically and overall a narrative—an immense, sprawling, capacious narrative.

This story contains forgiveness and heaven, but it also makes sense of life on earth. It gives us purpose. Living in and through it makes us truly human—as God intended. The language of "cooperative friends" acts as a shorthand, crib sheet, CliffsNotes way to understand our story. It is whole-life and active. It goes beyond mere beliefism or church life. It is centered in God.

As Jesus' cooperative friend, I live in alliance with what is already going on. I wake every day in an ongoing story. And in this story I play the role of God's cooperative friend. Jesus said:

> You are my friends when you do the things I command you. I'm no longer calling you servants because servants don't understand what their master is thinking and planning. No, I've named you friends because I've let you in on everything I've heard from the Father. (John 15:14-15)

Friends . . . I've let you in on everything. This amazing statement is easy to read without catching its full import. It's the basis of our cooperative friendship with Jesus. We get to be connected with Jesus in a similar way to how Jesus is linked with his Father. This "letting us in" business is at the heart of Jesus' grand design to involve us in carrying out the reclamation project of the Father. The grand scheme is often called the Great Commission, which is a charge to make apprentices of Jesus who live immersed in the trinitarian reality and who, as God's friends, do so for the sake of others.

THE GREAT COMMISSION TO MAKE COOPERATIVE FRIENDS

Jesus commissioned his friends on more than one occasion. But since the Great Commission is the best known, we'll look at it for a clue of what *friends* means and how Jesus' friends are created. The following passage is our master text on cooperative friendship with Jesus for the sake of others.

Jesus . . . gave his charge: "God authorized and commanded me to commission you: Go out and train everyone you meet, far and near, in this way of life, marking them by baptism in the three-fold name: Father, Son, and Holy Spirit. Then instruct them in the practice of all I have commanded you. I'll be with you as you do this, day after day after day, right up to the end of the age." (Matthew 28:18-20)

Jesus . . . gave his charge. *Charge*—or commission—is a serious word, not in a frightening way but in the sense that Jesus is speaking with clear and dynamic focus. He is highlighting the future activity of his friends. Jesus' words have the emotional power of the last words of a parent or grandparent on their death bed. They are words of instruction. They describe what his followers are to do in his physical absence but spiritual presence. Jesus' words powerfully confer authority on his followers. Jesus undoubtedly felt that nearly everything in his earthly life was over and there was one more vital concept to get across to his first followers.

God authorized and commanded me to commission you. This is a bit of background information from Jesus. It reminds me of the connect-the-dots games you see on kids' menus in a family restaurant. You've probably taken the crayon, connected all the dots and saw the elephant magically appear. Jesus is once again connecting this deployment to what the Father is doing. (Remember: "The Son can't independently do a thing, only what he sees the Father doing. What the Father does, the Son does" [John 5:19-20].) And note that he doesn't command us to create a new or separate religious life. Rather, we are to live in daily connection to the purpose of God and his story in order to lead others to be Jesus' followers.

In this commission Jesus is commanding us to cooperate with God in bringing our broken world into alignment with his purpose for creation. He is breaking the power of alternative stories and providing meaning for the world and all its inhabitants. He had been achieving this through Israel. Now, all peoples (Jews *and* Gentiles) are invited to join with him. Jesus' followers are called to partner with God in showing others how to be God's cooperative friends so that the world will be healed.

Go out and train everyone you meet, far and near. We carry out the Great Commission by training others. That might be an odd thought on first hearing. We might have expected Jesus to say, "Get people to pray *the prayer*" or "get people to believe in the virgin birth (or the resurrection or the doctrine of the Trinity)." I am not suggesting such doctrines are unimportant. But their true brilliance and importance is best understood in the context of becoming the cooperative friend of God, which includes being his agent of healing and generosity to others. Apart from this context, those doctrines are mere facts. Nice things, but they don't have the power to reorient life. Following Jesus is the only context in which such doctrines come alive and make one alive.

One more comment on the commission: most of us could rightly object—myself included—"But I can't really participate in the Great Commission, I am not a gifted evangelist." Here is a great piece of news: each of us has some gift, and any gift or talent can be leveraged on behalf of training others to follow Jesus. Hospitality, giving, verbal gifts, gifts of healing—they all matter when evangelism (making apprentices of Jesus) is in view, not just giving evangelistic talks. In the popular imagination evangelism has been reduced to gifted speakers speaking to large crowds. That leaves most of us out. However, coming alongside others to train them in a way of life lets all of us in on the adventure.

In this way of life. These five little words are powerful; they bring laser focus to the task of both following and making followers. As we've seen from the first few pages of this book, everything in Christianity is connected to life—"life and more life" as *The Message* puts it: life now, life in heaven, life at work, school and hobby. Learning a way of life is what it means to be a Christian. This is why the word *disciple*—which simply means learner—is such an important word in New Testament vocabulary. What are these learners learning? A way of life, a way of life in God as the cooperative friends of Jesus, carrying on his kingdom work of healing and redeeming the world.

I know that for me learning has been a nonstop process for more than thirty years. I am constantly learning new implications of Jesus' kingdom message. I consistently see areas of my life that need alignment with the kingdom. I am too worried about always getting things just right, always worried what others will think if I am wrong. I can be selfish in ways too awful to name. The other day I was wondering if some of my besetting sins will ever go away.

But none of that ultimately panics me or turns me inward. Jesus' followers have always struggled. Peter sure did. James and John had huge power issues ("Master, do you want us to call a bolt of lightning down out of the sky and incinerate them?" [Luke 9:54]). What they knew, and I have discovered, is that it's okay to learn alongside Jesus, our Master. I never find him to be mean or belittling. Rather, he is the embodiment of all the fruits of the Spirit—loving, patient, kind, generous and so forth (Galatians 5:22-23). This is what he charitably produces in his followers. So don't worry about this new kind of life being a drag—it is actually abundant life, life to the fullest, a movement toward full humanity as God intended.

Marking them by baptism in the threefold name: Father, Son and Holy Spirit. I resonate deeply with the way Dallas Willard talks about this marking by baptism. He says, and it strikes me as powerfully true, that this marking means something like "Immerse them in the triune reality." Two things are important here. First, this is not a story about an angry God who killed his Son. If the story is only about sin, heaven and hell, we can be forgiven for such a misunderstanding. But now we know it's a story about God and his kingdom, about a way of life in Jesus. Once we understand this, the third person of the

Trinity, the Holy Spirit, comes in view and is highly prized. Second, I love the idea conveyed by the word *immerse*. It expresses something much deeper than mere doctrine. It suggests being surrounded by the reality of God. Therefore when we are encircled by and immersed in the triune God, we are always safe. If we are going to live for others, this inner assurance of personal safety is a huge, must-have reality.

Then instruct them in the practice of all I have commanded you. This aspect of Jesus' charge gets us right to the core of being his co-operative friends. I suggest that an alternative word for "practice of all I have commanded you" is *cooperation*. The Great Commission is not about keeping a law and is not the fear-based pleasing of an angry God. Rather, it's like a young child pushing a little plastic mower while Dad mows the lawn. The child is thrilled at the thought of helping with the work—cooperating with what the parent is up to.

Training is the second important element of this phrase. Training and belief are related, but training is more fundamental, more profound. Christianity, being about a kind of life, is a practiced and embodied reality. In practice this looks more like apprenticeship, like gym instructors teaching students to develop a healthy life style, than classroom education. It seems to me that the process of instruction Jesus has in mind looks like learning an art or a sport—something you practice with pleasure because you love it.

I'll be with you as you do this, day after day after day, right up to the end of the age. Jesus' charge is not a new burden to add to a life that is already overbooked. He says that kingdom life, being yoked with him, is light and easy. Every command of Jesus comes with a promise: he will always be with us, empowering us, through the person and work of the Holy Spirit, which, of course, requires an interactive, ongoing conversational relationship with the Holy Spirit (see chap. 8).

Jesus' charge worked! It "took," as we say. It lit a fire in the hearts of his first friends. Trained by Jesus, they trained others in the way of

Jesus. Christianity spread throughout the known world like a wildfire driven by Santa Ana winds. Why? They did as Jesus said—they made followers, apprentices of Jesus, friends of Jesus, not mere members of a church.

FRIENDS OF JESUS ARE SENT BY JESUS

I rent an office above a very popular local hangout. It is an independent café. My Three Is Enough group (see chap. 10), which meets in the café, is just getting started. Right now it comprises a friend who works there and a friend of hers. It is a perfect place for us to learn to pay attention to others and the Holy Spirit. People are coming and going all day. Human drama unfolds all around us: baby showers, birthday parties, engagements, breakups, business deals, Bible studies, friends hanging out—you name it. It is a great field on which to practice cooperative skills.

The concept of agency is central to God's intention for his partners. Throughout history, God has exerted his will, power and authority through messengers, envoys, healers and sent ones. And Jesus is the ultimate sent one, the perfect cooperative friend of the Father. His incarnation models what it means to be sent into the world as God's renewed, Spirit-empowered people.

The Gospels' story is built around the idea of apostleship or being sent. Luke connects Jesus' self-conscious calling with his words to his first followers. Jesus told them, "Don't you realize that there are yet other villages where I have to tell the Message of God's kingdom, that this is the work God sent me to do?" (Luke 4:43). Jesus likewise sends his followers. Luke 9–10 recounts the sending of the disciples. And in John's Gospel we have these succinct words of Jesus: "Jesus repeated his greeting: 'Peace to you. Just as the Father sent me, I send you' " (John 20:21). He was sent and he sends us. In sending us, we become his apostles. This is the essential meaning of the Greek word *apostolos* and the Hebrew notion of *saliah:* a deputy commissioned and sent by another. From the opening story in the Garden to the pouring out of the Spirit at Pentecost, God's self-portrait is that of a "sending God." We live in an ongoing story of being "apostles," sent ones.

"APOSTLES" IN A CHANGING CULTURAL LANDSCAPE

I have placed the word *apostles* in parentheses because the term is often misunderstood. In my decades as a minister I have seen it both used well and abused. The word simply refers to a person who is sent with a message. In the popular imagination, apostleship, or one who has been sent, usually has a crosscultural connotation. The apostle Paul certainly is an example of being sent into a crosscultural context. A Hebrew by birth and a citizen of Rome, he was sent by God into the Greek milieu to minister among the Gentiles. He's now famous because his writings are recorded in Scripture. But in "real time" he was simply going to the neighborhoods God sent him. Though Thessalonica, Philippi, Athens, Corinth and Ephesus were culturally different from him, he nevertheless was sent to those places to deliver the message of the kingdom. In less visible and celebrated ways, this kind of calling and sending still happens today among God's people.

However, we do not need to go overseas or use a foreign language to be sent. We can be sent to our neighborhood, city and people. There is a desperate need for followers of Jesus to minister in our own changing landscape. Today, even though we were born and continue to live in the United States, many of us are living in a different culture—often called "postmodernism." As Bob Dylan sings, "The times, they are a-changin'."

We are sent into this often uncomfortable, crosscultural situation. We must go; we must love these people where they are, not where we wish they were. It will do no good to yell at or get preachy with them. Jesus said we are called to be a new kind of fishers, "catch[ing] men and women instead of perch and bass" (Matthew 4:19). One thing every fisher knows is that we catch fish on their terms, not ours! If they

only feed in the early morning, then you must get up early. If they eat
only certain bait, then that's what you must use.

The current cultural change is real, and "postmoderns" are real
people honestly struggling with real issues. Those of us who struggled with the 1960s sins of sex and drugs have no business getting
uppity with sincere people who have genuine questions about things
like truth. Over the last eight years I have spent a great deal of time
mentoring young adults—"sent ones"—who are conversing with
postmodern people. Mostly church planters, these men and women
are my heroes. They know they have been called and are sent; they
know how to be at peace and at ease in the new world. Their quiet,
unforced attitude is attractive to postmodern seekers. Seekers see in
such attitudes and body language that there is room for conversation
and ultimately for them.

SENT INTO POST-CHRISTENDOM

Post-Christendom describes the time period after the church was no
longer a central part of society. A simple way to capture this thought
is to picture in your mind a New England village with a "meeting
house" (church building) in the center of the town square; everything
else was built around it. From a psychological point of view, everyone knew they had to deal with the church. Everyone acknowledged
that the church and its leaders had authority. Except in rare settings,
this is no longer true in America. This is important because much of
what we assume about church and mission is based on the assumptions
of Christendom. Innovative people need to be sent into the post-
Christendom and post-Christian world.

When medieval Christendom merged with modernity in the eight-
eenth century, two explosive elements—like gasoline and fire—
came together. The merging of these two worldviews wasn't all bad;
it had its positives and negatives. There were both opportunities for
and threats to the gospel. Time does not allow a discussion of all the

virtues and faults of Christendom and modernity. I simply want to point out one change to our present social situation. In the world of modernity and Christendom, the average person expected religious experts to tell them what to think, what to do and how to "fix" people. That made sense. After all, the modern world demands and loves its experts. If our cars have a problem, we expect to find an expert mechanic to fix it. If we have a medical problem, we expect to find a doctor to fix us. Likewise, Christians looked to religious experts to solve their spiritual problems. With the passing of that worldview to postmodernity and a post-Christendom view, the institutional church and its experts were marginalized.

Today we are experiencing something akin to what John the Baptist, Jesus and Paul experienced in the pre-Christian world. While every era needs cooperative friends of Jesus, our culture needs Christ-followers—God-cooperative lives of service through the empowerment of the Holy Spirit—more than ever. This is the vision of the truly rewarding life of faith. No other vision will do. Certainly not a vision rooted merely in the hope of a good afterlife.

THE TENSION REGARDING INTENTION

The idea of cooperating with God, of being an ambassador of the kingdom, is often scary or negative. Some fear it will lead to works righteousness or legalism. Others fear that people will become self-appointed, power-abusing religious leaders. I understand the fear. Terrible harm has been done in the name of God. When we try to bring about the kingdom of God by our own force, all manner of evil can be released. Thus, just about everywhere I go these days I sense tension regarding the intention to be the cooperative friends of God. There's uneasiness about intentional evangelism and leadership. In most of the emerging, alternative church scene, it is not cool to enter a relationship with evangelism in mind or to lead a group toward a preferable future. But there is nowhere else to go. There is no legitimate place to run from our responsibilities as ambassadors of God. The answer to former evangelistic or leadership abuses is not to stay home or clam up. The answer is to go correctly—with a humble and serving attitude.

In many conversations I have, my talk of intentionally cooperating with God in evangelism and leadership is often taken to be manipulative. I understand the hesitation. I have seen the abuses. But, having thought about this a great deal, I want to offer a few tentative thoughts for a way forward. This is my honest attempt to interact with this new-fangled church conversation, with friends I have come to cherish. I want to stir up our imagination for leading, for growing as persons and for cooperation with God that avoids manipulation. I think I can show us a better way forward.

Let's start with some simple definitions.

- *Tension*—a state of psychological unrest and stress; a state of latent hostility or opposition

- *Intention*—a determination to act in a certain way; to aim at a target; the resolve to will something into being; to focus one's capacity to choose on an object or course of action

- *Manipulation*—to control or play upon another by artful, unfair or insidious means, especially to one's own advantage; in dealing with people, to give them an appearance of, but not a real choice in, a matter and to do so for selfish interests

Having been manipulated in many of our relationships, I think we all see the problem with manipulation. In fact, I'll bet you think we should doggedly stomp it out, especially when it relates to representing God, leading others or serving as a spiritual director.

The answer to misuse, usually in the form of manipulation, is not no use but *correct* use. If we want to live well, we can't live unintentionally. And despite the language to the contrary, no one is doing so. Those talking the loudest about "intention-free relationships" or "intention-free community" are actually envisioning and intending a course of action as well. They appropriately intend to discard or leave behind a negative—manipulation. They intend the absence of something. But stuff must be done, action must be taken, decisions must be made to implement that or any other vision. It's like wanting a trash-free yard: action is required, we must use our will, and we must regularly pick up the litter. So, let's just settle it: *We simply can't live without intention.* Made in the image of an intentional God, to be intention free simply is not a choice available to us.

Because manipulation is a polluter of being sent, just don't do it. Place manipulative tactics in your mind, circle them in red and draw a red line diagonally through the circle. A key for successfully leaving manipulation behind is finding security in eternal life in the kingdom of God. We usually manipulate and control out of insecurity and fear. The spiritual practice of considering others first (Philippians 2:3-8), rooted in the knowledge that we are always safe and taken care of in the kingdom, leads to the cure: freedom and generosity spills over to others.

We can be the cooperative friends of God if we are willing and able to do so in confident peace, leaving the results up to God and the person with whom we are relating. The "open secret" of the all too common mistreatment in churches—whether from pastor to people, people to pastor or people to people—is that one party is willing to do "whatever it takes to win." "Who cares about the cost?" these people say, "I want to win." At times a similar but subtler form of needing to win shows up in our evangelistic attempts. We simply can't have this attitude or the behaviors that spring from it. They must be set aside, or we will be forever stuck in deconstruction, hating the normal approach to leadership and evangelism but having no imagination or capacity for an alternative.

Here is a last big idea for moving forward without manipulation as the cooperative friends of Jesus: It's not about me or you; it's about

God and others. Envision leadership, evangelism and discipleship/ spiritual formation bathed in the Golden Rule and the Great Commandment. Do you feel freer with this as the way to proceed? I do. It fires my imagination for how to lead, share my faith and help others grow as people. It guides my intention to serve in ways that others around me are actually freer themselves, not less so. Whether correcting, dining, rebuking or attending a wedding, Jesus was himself utterly and totally free. As a man freed, safe in his Father's love, to be a servant, he freely loved others.

AN EXAMPLE FROM REAL LIFE

In the last community of faith I started and led in Southern California, I had a saying everybody was aware of and hopefully experienced: I do not want things *from* you; I want things *for* you. You will always be free to pursue the course that seems best to you and the Spirit. Such an attitude, and the actions that naturally spring from it, can remove the tension from the intention to be the cooperative friends of Jesus. Wanting things *for* others, not *from* them, spread in our church. For many of us it became a way of thinking about and doing life. To deepen our resolve and to equip ourselves for action, we as a whole community were excitedly reading materials from The Church of the Savior, Washington, D.C., and books by Dallas Willard, N. T. Wright, Richard Foster, Eugene Peterson and others like them. These authors helped shape our imagination, but the key was that we focused on that brief phrase. It's packed with real power and is able to impart a new imagination. In our collective mind we were going on the journey inward and the journey outward.

Let me give you an example. A couple of our families and a few single people lived in a nearby apartment complex. They banded together off and on throughout the week, sometimes just to hang out, sometimes to worship, sometimes to study or pray. But they adopted their apartment complex not only as the soil for their discipleship but also their mission in the world. They didn't just read about the mission groups of Church of the Savior, they formed one and sought to be ambassadors of the kingdom around the apartments. They didn't just read about Renovaré groups,* they banded together in an effort to express on behalf of their neighbors the six great traditions of the church: the prayer-filled life, the compassionate life, the virtuous life, the word-centered life, the spirit-powered life, and the sacramental life. They babysat for free; they invited neighbors for meals; they helped elderly people with chores, they hosted parties.

This may not seem like much—after all, anyone can do this! Furthermore, I don't mean to imply that this was a continuously spectacular ministry. But I do want you to see that being the cooperative friend of Jesus does not have to mean adding a bunch of religious stuff to an already too busy life. Friends of Jesus, seeking to live in creative goodness, do so best when it is within the typical routines of their life.

PRACTICES FOR COOPERATION

Over the last seventeen years I have taken seriously, with adaptation appropriate to my needs, the idea of spiritual disciplines. I have nothing new to say on this topic—I am a practitioner, not an original thinker. But I offer you a few pointers. The disciplines should be practiced in a targeted fashion. It's not good to start with a list of the disciplines and start practicing them randomly. Nor should we work from the top of the list to the bottom.

When I made the decision to live as a cooperative friend of Jesus, I took on some very simple disciplines that I could practice within my daily routines. For instance, as I am about to get on a conference call, I pray, "Father, may the words of my mouth and the mediations of my heart be acceptable in your sight on this call." Later, as I walk down

---

*Renovaré, founded by Richard Foster in 1988, has made a huge contribution to the practice of spiritual formation. See <www.renovare.org> for more information.

the hallway to a meeting, I pray, "Lord, may your kingdom come and may your will be done in this gathering."

No one notices me doing this. These prayers are offered silently while I dial a phone number, walk a few steps down a hallway or walk from my car to a restaurant. Because I can't prove it, I guess you'll have to trust me on this: these practices, and others like them, have transformed my heart and life. No big deal, no huge effort, but enormous return on investment.

I love the phrase *cooperative friend of Jesus*. It is the mental model I use for daily life. It summarizes the story in which I am seeking to be a faithful actor. I hope you come to love the idea too. In the next chapter I will say more about other practical things a cooperative friend of Jesus might do.

FOR REFLECTION AND DISCUSSION

1. Ephesians 2 says God has work for us to do. How would you answer a person who thinks working with Jesus is a new legalism or form of works righteousness?

2. *The Message* version of the Great Commission uses some powerful and image-rich terminology: "Go . . . train . . . in this way of life . . . instruct them in the practice." How does this new language inform your view of evangelism and discipleship?

3. The Christian story involves being sent. What do you think and how do you feel about being sent into our unsettled and transitioning society?

4. Have you ever felt the tension of intention in evangelism and leadership? If so, how did you or are you working through it?

CONSISTENT LIVES OF
CREATIVE GOODNESS

Apologetics of Another Kind

None of us will be measured on how much we accomplish
but on how well we love.

KRISTA TIPPETT, *SPEAKING OF FAITH*

Not long ago I was at a meeting of young pastors. The week before, I spoke at conference on evangelism at which a well-known apologist also spoke. Hearing about it my young friends began to tease me: "Why would anyone do that—have that person speak? No one relates to or appreciates apologetics anymore." They went on to explain to me that today many view apologetics as inherently dishonest; it purposely tells only one side of the story. Working hard to close the deal, they explained that "in the old days—like the last few decades—people valued being given the answers." "But not now," they went on, "people experience such an approach as manipulative or bullying."

Respected scholar John Stackhouse, who has written on "humble apologetics," puts it this way:

> [Ours] is a society suffused with the dynamics of irony and humor, keeping oneself from any final commitments and subverting the obvious, the standard, and the traditional so as to leave everything in play and nothing fixed, objective, and authoritative—except the freedom of individuals to pursue their own goals as they see fit. It is a society in which most people do not want to hear any simple, straight talk about Christianity: They already are Christians, or they "have heard it all before," or they even fear Christianity as sexist, homophobic, anti-environmentalist, imperialist, and other bad things. And it is a society in which we consumers are bombarded with attempts to claim our attention for this or that message, whether to eat at this particular restaurant in a couple of hours or to trust ourselves to that particular religion for all eternity. Our society, in sum, is leery, dubious, distracted, and jaded.

Apologetics, it seems, is dead. But I'm not buying it—at least not completely. I'll buy the fact that the dictionary definition of apologetics might have fallen on hard times—using formal logic, a systematic, argumentative discourse offering positive proof for or defenses of Christianity. It is true that people are tired of the worst forms of apologetics—being sold, spun and jerked around by selective logic. But that doesn't mean no one cares to know what is real, true or valid. It means that today many, but not all, people access truth and reality in ways that don't match up well with formal apologetics. A new form of apology, a new defense and explanation, is emerging. Contemporary seekers are often convinced of the reasonableness and beauty of faith in other ways. Witnessing a God-inspired, consistent life of creative goodness is, in my view, the new apologetic.

I suggest that creatively doing good for others is effective because lots of people today are not asking, Is this true? Rather, they tend to ask, Is it real, genuine and making a difference in your life? Are you becoming a better person because of your faith and the presence of God in your life? Do others experience you and your pursuit of religion as good for them? Seekers, at least those paying attention, have known too many people in their families, at work or around their neighborhoods who become worse as they pursue religion. Such people often become the office nag, the quarreling know-it-all, or the judgmental, gossipy neighbor.

Often, apologetics is believed—sometimes unfairly, to be sure—to fit a similar pushy, bossy mold. Again, this doesn't mean truth is irrelevant or that Christian doctrine is neither here nor there, but people access those things in different ways today than they have in the last few decades. And they often do so in a different order than what might be expected. Often, seeing that Christianity works, they then begin to look into various truths associated with Christianity.

OPENING HEARTS

Recently a friend of mine wrote me. Along with her church—a "missional community"—she is trying to live the kind of life we've been describing. She says:

> Our daughter was married not long ago. She and her husband-to-be insisted on having people sit together who did not know each other. As a result our Christian friends sat at tables with our friends that are still party animals. It was really amazing for both groups, as the Spirit blessed the whole event with camaraderie, and they had a great time with each other.
>
> At the wedding were friends from Chicago. They have recently become involved with a group that is on the fringes of Christianity. When they heard that we had become Christians, they were very standoffish. They were nervous about our new-

found belief systems, sure that we would try to convert them to our "tribe." We told them that we don't belong to a church, but rather a missional community that is more like a commando group. It's very small and we try to follow Jesus and try to act in response to what the Spirit starts, which is usually about showing love to others. Usually only one or two of us gets to "play" at a time and the others pray for whatever it is that is in motion.

All of the sudden our two friends opened up about how disillusioned they were with what they called "normal" church. They felt the church has become too large and money oriented. They wanted to know how we got the group together and what we thought about how they could start something similar. Hearing our story opened up a conversation that we would not have been able to have otherwise.

My point in recounting this story is not to bash "normal" churches (as my friend called them). A church of any size, shape or denomination can facilitate missional communities. My friends just happen to go to a small church that has several mission groups of three or four people. The point is that pursuing spiritual transformation and serving others under the leadership of the Holy Spirit opens the door of many hearts. Why? Today, many if not most church outsiders are suspicious and cynical. They're not ignorant of Christians and Christianity. They believe they have seen it, experienced it and, to them, have rightfully rejected it.

Aware of this reaction to church, we need to realize that being the cooperative friends of Jesus living for others is a powerful apologetic. Seeing an emerging pattern is not easy. We are accustomed to seekers following this model: first they believe Christian truth, then they join our churches, and then they take on our practices and behaviors. I suspect, though, that upon reflection we may see that people have come to faith in more varied ways. Today, many people are starting at the "end" and practicing their way into the faith. It seems to be working just fine. Others start in the middle by joining a Christian community before they believe. In fact, they often join in an effort to find out what Christians believe.

"The teacher appears when the student is ready." This saying contains great wisdom for contemporary evangelism. In an evangelistic exchange rooted in pursuing Christlikeness for the sake of others, the time will come when the seeker requests information, perhaps to refute a false claim or to unlock deeper faith. And the person providing the information is, in a sense, engaging in apologetics. When the information is sought from a trusted friend, the help provided doesn't feel like an annoying sales presentation; it is prized.

THE ULTIMATE PURPOSE OF GOD FOR HUMANITY

Last week, driving home from work, I saw a German shepherd running down a street near my house. Because it was windy that day, and my neighbor's gate often blows open, I was sure it was my neighbor's dog. I went over to his house to check on the gate. He saw me through the living room window and came out. I asked if his dog was home—and he was—all was good. As I turned to walk down his driveway, he said to me, "Man, I can't believe you would care about my dog." Then he asked, "When are you guys going to have another tamale party? I like being at your house."

For years my wife has had tamale-making parties during the New Year's holiday. We invite friends and neighbors and teach them how to make tamales out of cornmeal paste, various spiced meats, cheese, cornhusks and so on. We not only eat them but everyone gets to take a bunch home.

When I walk my own dogs and I see mail lying on the street, I take it to the correct residence. I keep my eyes open for any creative way to notice and serve others. Sometimes this leads to spiritual encounters, sometimes it doesn't.

Knowing the human tendency to reduce everything to its utilitarian value, we need to note that a life of creative goodness is right on its own terms. It's right because it is the ultimate purpose of the Creator for humanity. And there are lots of wonderful spillover effects. A long time ago the prophet Isaiah gave us a glimpse into God's desire that we cooperate with him in creative goodness for the sake of others.

First, Isaiah gives us an imagination for the kinds of actions and attitudes that express creative goodness:

> Break the chains of injustice,
> get rid of exploitation in the workplace,
> free the oppressed,
> cancel debts.

> What I'm interested in seeing you do is:
> sharing your food with the hungry,
> inviting the homeless poor into your homes,
> putting clothes on the shivering ill-clad,
> be available to your own families. (Isaiah 58:6-7)

Looking after a neighbor's dog, picking up lost mail and making tamales don't quite get to the level of Isaiah's vision, but through these small practices I hope to get there some day. It is fascinating to me that God has created this to be the ultimate, nonutilitarian, win-win situation. It is obvious that those who receive help are blessed. What is less obvious and less experienced is that Christians who live creative lives of goodness are blessed. Isaiah says:

> If you get rid of unfair practices,
> quit blaming victims,
> quit gossiping about other people's sins,
> If you are generous with the hungry
> and start giving yourselves to the down-and-out,

Your lives will begin to glow in the darkness,
    your shadowed lives will be bathed in sunlight.
I will always show you where to go.
    I'll give you a full life in the emptiest of places—
    firm muscles, strong bones.
You'll be like a well-watered garden,
    a gurgling spring that never runs dry.
You'll use the old rubble of past lives to build anew,
    rebuild the foundations from out of your past.
You'll be known as those who can fix anything,
    restore old ruins, rebuild and renovate,
    make the community livable again. (Isaiah 58:9-12)

Though I can't give an exhaustive list of all the reasons God made humankind, I'll list a couple that come to mind.

It works something like this: tonight at dinner, my daughter lifted her bare foot in the air to show me a cut she had on her big toe. While at it, she commented—I should say she lamented—that she "has my feet." Then she placed her palm against mine and compared them. Again, they were very much the same. Poor girl, she got the low end of the gene pool among parental appendages! And on occasions when I've met my son's colleagues and friends, they have commented, "Jonathan's attitudes and mannerisms are just like yours!"

It is God's nature to create and do good through his creation. It is like that with us too. Bearing his image (Genesis 1:27), we are bent in the same direction—toward creative goodness. God's traits are in us. Sometimes those good traits are buried, but they are there nonetheless. That's really the place to start: being a Christian means to live an others-oriented life of creative goodness; it's central to God's character. One definition of sin, then, is to live a selfish life that harms others. Such a life misses the target, chooses a wrong path and willfully ignores our God-given wiring.

GOD'S RESCUE MISSION

God is on a rescue mission. It wasn't always that way. In the beginning neither the first humans nor the Garden needed to be fixed—all was well. All the humans had to do was cooperate with God in the rhythms of the sin-free creation. But the earthquake of sin changed everything. Both in their relationship to God and in general ethical terms, humanity tumbled down like an old brick building in a big California shaker. God raised up Abraham and Israel as his agents of rescue. But, as N. T. Wright has memorably put it, the firemen became arsonists. Throughout its history, Israel made contributions to the seismic tension underlying earthquakes. This is what Isaiah brought to their attention.

The Christian church has a mixed history as well. All of us have failed as God's cooperative friends—the first humans, Israel and the church. God's plan is that we creatively partner with him in digging humanity out from that rubble, that we invent new tools, discover paths which lead to freedom and shed light in the darkest, most hopeless underground entrapments. This is the life of creative goodness.

For those trying to follow God's ways, knowing what he is up to naturally leads to cooperation. This is why I love the phrase *cooperative friends of Jesus*. Isaiah's words give us the outline of what lives of cooperation might look like. If we employ or supervise people, it means treating them fairly, insuring that their relationship with us is experienced as good. It means not acting religious and harming others. Most profoundly, it means feeding the hungry, sheltering the homeless, clothing the ill-clad, being available to our own families, stopping unfair practices, protecting victims, and refusing to gossip about others.

When we cooperate with Jesus in these ways, our lives will begin to glow in the darkness. This is a different kind of apologetics. Yes, we still need verbal witness, and yes, the truth still matters. But in our 24/7 spin me, sell me, manipulate me, exploitative world, actions speak louder than words for millions of seekers.

These social justice activities are often done in the poor part of town or overseas. Thus they are divorced from the routines of our daily life. My hope is that the heart of those who work in social justice will spread dramatically to those of us who do not go overseas—or even across town. In reality, we all go. We go to work, to school and to places where we have authentic community—our neighborhood, the gym and clubs of various kinds.

What if we could bring together the actual events and people of our daily life with a heart like those who go overseas and across town to be the people of God as envisioned by Isaiah? In addition to the obvious goodness that others would receive, in addition to repairing the negative image of Christianity, we would find ourselves in the bull's-eye of Jesus's vision for his followers. Jesus said:

I was hungry and you fed me,
I was thirsty and you gave me a drink,
I was homeless and you gave me a room,
I was shivering and you gave me clothes,
I was sick and you stopped to visit,
I was in prison and you came to me. (Matthew 25:35-36)

Christians are fundamentally connected to lives of creative goodness—that *is* what we do. We love—that is, we seek the good of others—whether at home or out-and-about in all the activities of our normal lives. We do it for several reasons.

First, it is what God desires for his people—to serve his creation as his agents, as ambassadors of his kingdom. This is the fidelity the prophets regularly called Israel to. In the eyes of the prophets, *being* Israel was far more important than what we now think of as doctrine or theology. Right belief is always in the service of right attitudes and actions. Belief is never trumpeted as superior. In Scripture we never find the notion that action would be great—if we get around to it—but right belief is the most important thing! I don't recall Israel being up-

braided for failing to articulate a theory about the burning bush, how
aged Sarah and Elizabeth bore children, or how the water piled up for
them but fell on the Egyptians. On the other hand, God's people are
often reminded of their calling to be his agents of rescue on behalf of
the last, the least and the lost.

Second, caring for others pleases God—even brings glory to him.
Third, it is good for others. Fourth, it is good for us—living this way
we become humanity as God intended. Last, a community of faith living in creative goodness on the behalf of others may be the most powerful demonstration of the gospel, the most effective form of evangelism in contemporary society. Let's look at this last point.

One weekend, I read a manuscript for a friend; in it he related
the story of a teenager who honestly, if not shockingly, said, "Being
a Christian is like having a bad job. You do it for the money, but you
hate it the whole time." What experiences led this young person to
that conclusion? It's safe to say that Christianity is no storied journey
for him. I wonder if he meant this: *money*, for him, corresponded to
forgiveness and heaven, but Christian life is a total bore—no story, no
adventure, no spiritual gifts, no contribution, no partnering with God
in his rescue operation.

Living a consistent life of creative goodness, on the other hand,
pulls the best out of us. We feel fully alive, fully human. This kind of
life is good for us. In it we become most human—truly us. We are
fully human while expressing constant goodness on behalf of others.
This story sets the trajectory for our eternal destiny and undying cosmic role. The apostle John says that ultimately we are going to rule
and reign with God for all eternity in the renewed heaven and earth
(Revelation 22:5).

SIN: CREATIVE GOODNESS CAN'T GO THERE
"You put us in charge of your handcrafted world, repeated to us your
Genesis-charge" (Psalm 8:6). In God's charge, repeated by leaders and

prophets throughout the ages through images like "salt and light" and "a nation of priests," God depicts humanity's role in the cosmos: to be his cooperative friends, caring about what he cares about, which is *all* creation. God cares about the planet, about systemic injustice and poverty, about the eternal destiny of humans. You don't need to choose one over the others. Rather, we are called to cooperate daily with God in whatever comes our way. Work to make just laws. Help those in need. Pick up trash. If someone has questions about spiritual things, converse in peace, without needing to win an argument.

We've made being good to others too difficult. Some of us have confused ourselves into apathy. Sometimes we have theological hang-ups about "what really counts." For many Christians of my generation, "saving souls for eternity" is what really counts. Everything else is optional, but mostly viewed as a distraction from the real thing. Now, the pendulum seems to be swinging the other way. To an increasing degree, we are losing the ability and confidence to share our faith, to help someone decide to be a follower of Jesus. We are not sure why we should do it. Both heaven and hell are like long-lasting fads that are going out of fashion. Sin is increasingly minimized by all sorts of psychotherapeutic, cultural and pop alternatives.

Sin is a plain concept: it means to miss the mark, the target, the aim and intention of God for us. I don't think anyone would argue the run-of-the-mill sins are in continuity with God's will. We, along with our culture, may be confused about issues of sexuality, but we don't like being lied to, stolen from or abused. Sin is still sin, after all. Sin harms the sinner and those sinned against. It harms our relationships, most importantly our relationship with God—which makes necessary reconciliation through Christ. Sin runs contrary to God's Genesis charge, don't you think?

The normal, and perhaps sincere, excuse "I'm way too busy to focus on others" doesn't hold up in light of God's charge and what it means to be a Christian—a Christlike person. Acting with and encouraging justice—whether at work, home, school or wherever—doesn't make us busier. But it does display the character of God and fulfills our destiny as God's image-bearers. It takes seconds to pick up trash from a neighbor's yard, and even less to greet a street person. You've got to have lunch anyway, why not take a relational risk by inviting that coworker who is taking steps toward faith. Who knows where the conversation will lead?

FINDING YOUR TRUE SELF

Viewing the Christian story in this manner (cooperative friends/ creative goodness) provides us with an ironic and subversive way to explain the gospel. It is ironic because though old, it sounds new and fresh. It is subversive because it twists things just enough to allow the cynical and wary to give it a new hearing. It allows us to demonstrate the gospel's goodness and its relevance to contemporary life.

A few years ago I started a community of faith designed to work with young people—and some older people—who were struggling with God, Christianity and church. Many of these people were deeply hurt, confused and cynical. Had I tried to sing the same old song or, worse, to defend it, we would have gotten nowhere. But many of these young people found their way back to God, back to following Jesus. In part, they responded positively because we rethought some of the things we did in community. Rethinking is a little nerve-racking for a conservative guy like me. I was able to keep going because at virtually every step I could see that, far from compromising, we were discovering something old which was exciting and adventurous.

For many of my young friends, Christianity seemed to be a life-shriveling reality. As we found our way to cooperative friendship and creative goodness, we all learned that serving others as ambassadors of God's kingdom is the path to being our best selves; it is the way, through the grace of God in Christ, to be humanity as God intended. Jesus, sending his first followers into precisely this kind of life, said,

"When you enter a town . . . heal anyone who is sick, and tell them, 'God's kingdom is right on your doorstep!' " (Luke 10:8-9).

Earlier, Jesus told his friends what they could expect for themselves as they followed him into his kind of God-centered, others-oriented life:

> Anyone who intends to come with me has to let me lead. You're not in the driver's seat—I am. Don't run from suffering; embrace it. Follow me and I'll show you how. Self-help is no help at all. Self-sacrifice is the way, my way, to finding yourself, your true self. What good would it do to get everything you want and lose you, the real you? (Luke 9:23-25)

"Finding your true self" sounds so New Age, doesn't it? Well, Jesus knew what he was talking about long before the "new age" started in the twentieth century! Sadly, while many of us have been bashing the hearts of seekers as they struggle to find a way to experience God, we forgot to tell them that they could follow Jesus and they would find him good. They'd find God *and* their true selves, and it would be good for others as well.

THE GOLDEN TRIANGLE OF PRESENCE

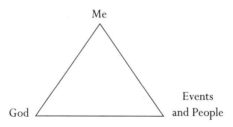

I use a mental model to simultaneously keep focused on my growth in Christ and on my calling as an ambassador of the kingdom. It is extraordinarily simple. I pay attention to and stay present to God and to the people and events of my daily life. I call this practice "the Golden Triangle of Presence." As I go through my day, I seek to be truly present to what is going on around me: the people I am with or the work I am doing, and to the voice of God. The three points of the triangle are "Me," the "Events and People" of my life, and "God." I hold them together by paying attention, by simultaneously being aware of all three aspects. God has given us the capacity to do this. Having multiple focus points isn't difficult. It's as if one ear is attuned to God and the other to the activities and people of my life. With practice, it doesn't even seem like multitasking. Every time I see my daughter listening to her iPod while text messaging on her cell phone, carrying on a MySpace conversation and doing homework (she's an A student) with the TV on, I know I can practice my little triangle of presence. What is harder than the actual practice is the will to do it. But once I get that part right, God, through the Spirit, enables the remainder of the process.

Dallas Willard thinks of God's guidance in the triangle as "the still small voice." He says "the very phrase 'the still small voice' might seem to suggest that what lies at the heart of a relationship with God is something weak and marginal. But that is far from the truth. One who hears God's voice is operating from the very foundation and framework of all reality, not from the fringe." Hearing this voice requires our careful attention because our own wants, neuroses and activities as well as the people and dealings of life scream at us so loudly. They overwhelm us with their presence, making the spiritual part of the triangle seem unreal. "The visible world daily bludgeons us with its things and events. They pinch and pull and hammer away at our bodies. . . . But instead of shouting and shoving, the *spiritual* world whispers at us ever so gently."

Habitually paying attention to God, through the Spirit, is a fundamental attitude and practice for life in the kingdom for the sake of others. It tunes us in to ourselves, our life and the presence of God. Being alert to God is essential for our own growth and our missional encounters in the world. Silence and solitude are two of the spiritual disciplines most practiced in the history of the church. They enable us to hear the voice of God in any setting. As we practice paying attention in silence and solitude, we learn to hear God's voice in the hurry and busyness of life. Willard says, "God comes to us precisely in and through our thoughts, perceptions and experiences." "He can approach our conscious life *only* through them, for they are the substance of our lives." "Generally speaking, God will not compete for our attention."

Occasionally, someone like Saul (later Paul) gets knocked to the ground, but in most cases God won't run over us. In fact, "God's spiritual invasions into human life seem by their very gentleness almost to invite us to explain them away." Because this is so easy to do, many seekers and Christians succeed in explaining away God's overtures to them.

> We are hindered in our progress toward becoming spiritually competent people by how easily we explain away the movements of God toward us. They go meekly, without much protest. . . . But for now he cooperates with the desires and inclinations that make up our character. . . .
>
> [I]f, by contrast, we are ready and set to find ways of explaining away his gentle overtures, he will rarely respond with fire from heaven. More likely he will simply leave us alone.

Now there is a truly sobering thought. That would be my version of hell on earth. Thus there is no way to live for the sake of God and others without an ongoing, interactive relationship with God.

All of our daily existence is the grounds for and focus of discipleship. Our apprenticeship to Jesus must focus on our actual life; this is crucial. The actions associated with discipleship can't be added to an overly busy life. The opposite is true. Paying attention to God in the actual routines of life is the heart of discipleship. This injects all of life— job, school, neighbors, family—with meaning. It breaks the harmful sacred-secular dualism that plagues contemporary Christianity.

To those outside the church, such dualism, which leads to acting one way in church and another in the world, is rank hypocrisy. Willard correctly says, "If we restrict our discipleship to special religious times, the majority of our waking hours will be isolated from the manifest presence of the kingdom in our lives." To outsiders that isolation makes Christianity look empty, colorless and irrelevant.

But when we live for the sake of others within the ebb and flow of our days, something changes. People are curious about anyone working for the good of others. This is what explains, at least partially, the fascination with home makeover shows, pop-idol adoptions and celebrity advocacy of various social issues. Cooperative friends of Jesus living in creative goodness for the sake of others are in prime position to reveal the person and work of God in our world.

FOR REFLECTION AND DISCUSSION

1. Do you think others-oriented goodness is a powerful apologetic for the Christian faith? Why or why not?

2. Being a partner in God's rescue mission on the earth is a new way to think about what it means to be a Christian. How could you partner with God this week?

3. Isaiah 58:9-12 says that acting with God has potent spillover effects. Give some examples of when you have seen this work.

4. Imagine yourself practicing the Golden Triangle of Presence. Give a couple of examples of how this would work in your life.

FOR THE SAKE OF OTHERS

Jesus Could Have Done Backflips on a Donkey

Christ has set us free to live a free life. . . .
It is absolutely clear that God has called you to a free life.
Just make sure that you don't use this freedom as an excuse
to do whatever you want to do and destroy your freedom.
Rather, use your freedom to serve one another in love;
that's how freedom grows. For everything we know about God's Word
is summed up in a single sentence: Love others as you love yourself.
That's an act of true freedom.

GALATIANS 5:1, 13-14

I love the simplicity of the following story. It illustrates the uncompli-
cated and fun way we can tie together the themes of this book—being
cooperative friends of Jesus by doing creative good for the sake of
others. A group of friends in a church organized themselves into little
mission groups. This is one of their stories.

We were part of a church that had a ministry to unwed teen-age mothers who needed diapers. The girls would come once a month and get diapers and formula. We would offer free hair-cuts and manicures to pamper them. I said to one of the girls, "Gosh, I bet you're excited about summer coming." She replied, "Like that's going to make a difference in my life."

It started me thinking about what it was that I liked so much about summers when I was a young mother. With that in the back of my mind, my daughter's college roommate came over one evening and started talking about how she had to get in shape for her summer job as a Mommy and Me swimming in-structor for the Red Cross. At that moment it became clear that the Spirit had something special in mind. We went to the pastor to discuss our idea to give girls swimming lessons at his house. He was naturally full of concerns. We said we would gladly host the lessons at our pool. He still had concerns about the church being sued if it were connected with the lessons. One of the founding members of the church was our insurance agent who assured us we could not be sued if we didn't charge anything. We decided to do it on our own. The pastor allowed us to hand out flyers at the next diaper giveaway.

We began preparation for the lessons by talking about it with our small group. It became one of our outreaches. We all prayed and begin asking the Spirit to take charge and lead us. The first week only one mom came with her daughter. We had prepared a large barbeque meal for any families that might at-tend. Our friend taught the swimming lesson while the rest of us stood around the edge of the pool encouraging and cheering for the baby girl. We had lunch and laughter after the lesson, and learned a lot about our guest and her daughter. The next time we had three moms and three babies. We had silly blow-up toys for the children as prizes for a water-induced, nerve-wracking job well done. We sat down for a great barbeque and got to know each girl's story. The last week we had about fifteen, because the fathers of the kids and other family came.

Each week we would pray for the Spirit to fill the house with his love and his peace. Our group prayed for great conversations with our new friends and for God's will to be done at the lessons. We had a great time. Although Christ was not discussed every time, we all felt his love and acceptance. We have developed a friendship with the teacher and her husband. We are going to watch him play soccer tomorrow. They are not Christians yet, although they did invite us to see their daughter baptized.

We all thought the swim lessons were a huge success, even though there was no one was converted and only one lasting friendship was formed. We've been taught that our role is to develop authentic friendships, to serve others in these simple ways and to pray for them. We can be at peace in this. Jesus wants people to follow him more than we want them to, and he will do the heavy work with them. We have been taught that kingdom work is done mostly on your knees talking to God, which is part of our inward journey. Our outward journey involves using our ears by listening to people and relies heavily on the leading of the Holy Spirit. Our job is to love the people he places in our lives and be the kind of Christians they can trust when they are ready to talk about faith.

JESUS FOR THE SAKE OF OTHERS

Tom Wright writes that "Jesus is lifted up to draw us all to himself, and to enable us to be for the world what he was for the world. . . . [T]he whole amazing story of Jesus, with all its multiple levels, is given to us to be our story as we follow him." Jesus of course is lifted up most poignantly on the cross, redeeming humanity. But, crucial to our imagination for being the cooperative friends of Jesus for the sake of others, his whole life is lifted up as a model. It is abundantly clear that sacrifice is the core and the foundation of Jesus' life. Sacrifice is therefore a model for those followers who would come after Jesus.

Here is a simple way to imagine such a life for ourselves: Think of an elementary school teacher holding up the project of one fifth-grader and saying, "This is what your assignment needs to look like." The teacher is saying, this is the way things are supposed to be, copy this, use this as a pattern to follow. For our purposes we might say, Look at Jesus' life, copy him, mold your life to him. While we can't do what he did on the cross (he alone is the Savior), we can shape our lives for the sake of others, as he did.

In this chapter we will first look at how Jesus sought the good of others. Then we will look at Paul's vision for how this might happen in us.

In the small village of Nain, which ironically derives its name from the Hebrew word for pleasant, a young, widowed mother was experiencing a horrific event, her son's funeral. As Jesus came into the town, he was stopped by the funeral procession. Jesus' heart broke. He comforted the mother, touched the coffin and raised the boy to life! Then Luke adds:

> They all realized they were in a place of holy mystery, that God was at work among them. They were quietly worshipful—and then noisily grateful, calling out among themselves, "God is back, looking to the needs of his people!" The news of Jesus spread all through the country. (Luke 7:16-17)

"God is back, looking to the needs of his people!" And the news spread. This is how the rule and reign of God ought to be experienced among us today. *Caring for the needs of others* is what I have in mind, not just the spectacular part about the boy's resuscitation. I like the thought of others experiencing Christianity "for their good." But because of two dynamics, Christianity is seldom seen as being good for others. First, many Christians believe that our relationship with God is a private matter—just between Jesus and me. Second, when we do extend our beliefs into the public sphere, we are noted for nagging, for being judgmental, argumentative or holier than thou.

But we see neither of these in Jesus. His relationship to the Father was a public matter and resulted in loving and serving others. And Jesus was not into self-aggrandizement. If he wanted to draw attention to himself or to display his divinity, he could have done backflips on a donkey down Nain's (or Jerusalem's) main street! Instead, he demonstrated the presence of the kingdom by serving others. We demonstrate the presence of God in our life the same way—by doing good for the sake of others.

This is our pattern. True religion, at its heart, is about the Other and others. I like the way a bumper sticker puts it: Only one six-billionth is about me! Public Radio's Krista Tippett, speaking of religion in general, gives us valuable guidance:

> The context of all virtue in the great religious traditions is relationship—relationship with God, practical love in families and communities, care for the "other." They insist on reverent attention to the outcast and the suffering and the stranger beyond the bounds of one's own identity. Christianity puts an extreme fine point on this, calling also for love of enemies. These qualities of religion should enlarge, not narrow, our public conversation on all of the important issues before us. They should reframe it.

Seeing ourselves as cooperative friends of Jesus is step one. Seeking to constantly live in creative, healing goodness is the logical next step. Seeing the need for the filling and empowering of the Holy Spirit naturally follows too. But why do those three things? Not to earn favor from God. Not to gain esteem from others. Like Jesus, we do it for the sake of others. Jesus, we could say, existed for the world. The church too exists for and lives in solidarity with the world. This is what it means to love God and love our neighbor.

USE YOUR HEADS

The apostle Paul, in the letter to the Colossians, gives us a vision, an outline for how life for the sake of others might actually be accomplished. He writes:

> Use your heads as you live and work among outsiders. Don't miss a trick. Make the most of every opportunity. Be gracious in your speech. The goal is to bring out the best in others in a conversation, not put them down, not cut them out. (Colossians 4:5-6)

First, let's think about the context for Paul's comments. For the Christ-followers in Colossae, the big battles of the everyday grind of life had been won in Jesus. Jesus is victorious! He delivered them from oppressive superstitions regarding the gods. They knew that he is Lord; he defeated the principalities and powers. Life was now different, especially for those held down by the political, religious, economic and spiritual powers. They had hope, death was defeated, and the psychological and spiritual weight of sin was lifted. The woman at the well, the woman caught in adultery, and the tax collectors Zacchaeus and Levi are examples of those for whom connection with Jesus meant a new life.

Earlier in the letter Paul describes this new freedom, saying, "God rescued us from dead-end alleys and dark dungeons. He's set us up in the kingdom of the Son he loves" (Colossians 1:13). I love the lines in one of Anne Lamott's books: "Lies cannot nourish or protect you. Only freedom from fear, freedom from lies, can make us beautiful, and keep us safe. There is a line, I try to live by: . . . 'And may the free make others free.' "

The great hope for Paul is that this freedom—in all the ways it affects this life and the next—would spread to others. We call this spreading "evangelism." By this point in the book, I hope you agree with me that evangelism entails more than words—that faith in and following Jesus spreads as the cooperative friends of Jesus live in creative goodness for the sake of others through the animating and empowering presence of the Holy Spirit. In Colossians 4:5-6, Paul gives us both a value system to work from and some practical advice. Let's have a look at the passage bit by bit.

Use your heads. This means that we should be present and alert to our life, to God and to the people and events of our life. This is neither hard nor particularly spiritual. It means something like "be aware, be attentive."

As you live and work among outsiders. Some converts in Colossae were tempted to secede from the world, to conceal themselves in what we might call secret societies—perhaps something like freemasonry or the Order of Skull and Bones. Their motivation was to protect themselves and their new faith from run-of-the-mill people and the pollution those people might bring to the new community. For Paul this manner of thinking is completely backward. It is contrary to the incarnation of Jesus, the way God connected with polluted human beings.

To combat this temptation Paul reminded them that the normal routines of life, the people and events that make our communities, matter. These are spiritual. We don't need to add "spiritual" activities to our life as much as we need to make our actual, everyday life spiritual. What we typically think of as "spiritual" often ends up creating a false dualism. Usually we aren't even conscious of the false dualism we fall into. A default setting leads us to think that there are two realities: our *real* life (work, school, friends, kids, dating, playing) and our *spiritual* life (praying, reading the Bible, meditating, going to church, practicing spiritual disciplines). Paul instructed the Colossians to live in solidarity with the world as it is.

Don't miss a trick. Make the most of every opportunity. Here Paul encourages us to live constant lives of creative goodness. We don't want to miss any opportunity; even small things matter. But in taking every opportunity to do good, we must not bring attention to ourself, manipulate others or cause them to feel indebted to us in any way. We are simply looking for genuine, altruistic ways to be good to others.

Be gracious in your speech. What is gracious speech? It is others-oriented. It asks, What will these words do to my hearer? Gracious speech seeks the good of others. It exhibits Paul's attributes of love:

> Love cares more for others than for self.
> Love doesn't want what it doesn't have.
> Love doesn't strut,
> Doesn't have a swelled head,
> Doesn't force itself on others,
> Isn't always "me first,"
> Doesn't fly off the handle,
> Doesn't keep score of the sins of others,
> Doesn't revel when others grovel, . . .
> Always looks for the best. (1 Corinthians 13:4-7)

Gracious speech doesn't judge whether someone is worthy of our generosity. Our grace to others mirrors God's grace to us: unmerited and free of charge.

The goal is to bring out the best in others. We act and speak for the sake of others with the goal that they'll know we are interested in their good. This—bringing out the best in others—is central to the vision I am commending.

In a conversation. Respect—listening to others, really hearing them, connecting with what they are saying even if we do not agree—is at the heart of this passage. Seekers need to feel our solidarity with them, just as Jesus is in solidarity with us. This is not advocating thoughtless and meaningless relativism. Rather, I want to highlight the obvious fact that our conversation partners see only what they see. We must start where they are, with graciousness and genuine love, willing their good at every turn, not where we wish they were.

Our conversations with others can be seasoned or "kicked up a notch," as the famous chef Emeril Lagasse says, by showing genuine interest, that is, paying attention to others' stories, being alert to their hopes and fears, doubts and challenges.

[Do] not put them down, [do] not cut them out. What putdowns do we engage in? Research done by David Kinnaman, president of the Barna Group, gives insight into how young outsiders to the church view Christianity, what "cuts them out":

> Many of those outside of Christianity, especially younger adults, have little trust in the Christian faith, and esteem for the lifestyle of Christ followers is quickly fading among outsiders. . . .
>
> [The] most common reaction to the faith: they think Christians no longer represent what Jesus had in mind, that Christianity in our society is not what it was meant to be. . . . They admit they have a hard time actually seeing Jesus because of all the negative baggage that now surrounds him. . . .
>
> The growing hostility toward Christians is very much a reflection of what outsiders feel they receive from believers. They say their aggression simply matches the oversized opinions and egos of Christians. One outsider put it this way: "Most people I meet assume that *Christian* means very conservative, entrenched in their thinking, antigay, antichoice, angry, violent, illogical, empire builders; they want to convert everyone, and they generally cannot live peacefully with anyone who doesn't believe what they believe." . . .
>
> It is important to realize that young outsiders attribute their image of Christianity primarily to conversations and firsthand experiences. . . .
>
> Many of these young people actually went through a time when they were searching for faith. They were probing the Christian faith, trying it on for size, but they couldn't get past some of the

mental, emotional, or spiritual barriers—often heightened by their experience of an unChristian faith—so they gave up. This should be a major wake-up call for us.

Humanly speaking, the American church may be at a make-it or break-it point for introducing outsiders to Jesus. Paul says that we need to make the most of every opportunity, be gracious in our speech, bring out the best in others in our conversations, not putting them down, not cutting them out. This is the right thing to do.

WHY BE GOOD?

"Now, be good." "Play nice." Every child has heard these words. Sometimes, a child sarcastically replies, "Why?" But is it merely sarcastic? I think that most people—young and old—simply don't have compelling, life-organizing reasons for being good, for acting with God and others in mind, for keeping the Golden Rule ("Do to others as you would have them do to you" [Luke 6:31 NIV]) or the Great Commandment (" 'Love the Lord your God with all your heart and with all your soul and with all your strength and with all your mind'; and, 'Love your neighbor as yourself' " [Luke 10:27 NIV]).

I can imagine adults sincerely wondering, *Why are God and others foremost, central?* Over the past few centuries we have been indoctrinated with Enlightenment individualism. Living as autonomous selves rationally looking out for our own interests is embraced as the only way to live, to get what we deserve, to be secure.

The default position of "me first" is simply too strong. Looking out for number one—with an occasional condescending tip of the hat to God, a neighbor or coworker—is to contemporary moral thought what gravity is to physics: unquestioned. And even if it were questioned, people would wonder, *Where would I possibly get the motivation and the moral energy to serve others first? To be different than I currently am, I would need a rocket engine to lift that payload off the launching pad.*

The social changes presently at play make a coherent ethical life difficult. Today, "right and wrong" are neither easy to know or do. Previous consensus on such matters has buckled under the pressure of the relativism, pluralism and secularism of post-Christian America. But something even more profound is going on here than the lack of ethics or moral energy. We lack moral imagination. We need a story that, like a washing machine, can agitate us, clean us and spin us around a few times. Then, when we are hung out to dry, the Spirit can blow his fresh and empowering wind through us. Our moral imagination will then be refreshed, renewed.

We need an imaginative way forward, one rooted in a positive and holistic vision, not in negative prohibitions. I suggest that the story of God's kingdom-based partnership with humanity is the best way to articulate a Christian ethic in our post-Christian era. We need a story that is both inspiring and normative, that leads to a healthy focus on others as the way to be fully human, fully alive.

IS THE CHURCH GOOD?

When I was a young leader in the mid-1970s, our biggest concern was to make church relevant, cool, hip and understandable to our generation. Along with taking out pews, stained-glass windows and various symbols from the sanctuary, perhaps the biggest change was using contemporary Christian music: folk-rock music with straightforward Christian lyrics. While this seems completely benign now, at the time it was a serious ethical controversy. Some said that such music was of the devil, while others retorted, "Why should the devil have all the good music?" It seems so quaint now.

Today, we have a completely different set of questions being asked. Few people today are concerned with making the church cool or popular. They are asking ethical questions about the church. They wonder whether the church is a force for good or evil on earth. When many young people think of the church, they think of people who hate gays and oppress women, and who force their opinions on others in impolite or even coercive ways. Because of this George Barna notes that there are twenty million *sincere believers* who no longer want to have anything to do with church.

Perhaps most painfully, they think of atrocious double standards, which make Christians seem selfish at best and dishonest at worst. During the last decade I have heard young people tell stories of being kicked out of church for drug use or sexual sin while others in the church kept their leadership positions—even though their own flagrant sins were widely known. These young people also see the church acting wholly without grace toward others. In many cases they see no point in trying to be an authentically good person—even if they could figure out what that means.

In the past my colleagues and I assumed a definite context for talking about ethics. We knew the biblical stories from our Sunday school lessons. Though not expressively kingdom-centered or rooted in a deep understanding of God's covenant with Israel, the stories we learned gave us reasons for "being good." This basis of moral knowledge can no longer be assumed. Our culture doesn't have a basis for a moral life; there is no moral vision. Our ethical imagination must be shaped by a story. We love stories. We crave a story that will inspire us, a story so big that it embraces all of life and allows us to thrive. God's story, his intention for humanity as expressed in his covenant with Israel and the kingdom life of Jesus, does just that.

DIVINE-HUMAN PARTNERSHIP FOR THE SAKE OF OTHERS

The biblical term *covenant* implies a divine-human partnership initiated by God. The concept of covenant is powerful. It can shape our imaginations for being God's people—which means we exist for others. Old Testament scholar John Bright reveals that covenant is not an ivory-tower idea but is truly earthy and practical:

Though Israel's notion of God was unique in the ancient world, and a phenomenon that defies rational explanation, to attempt to understand her faith in terms of an idea of God would be a fundamental error. Israel's religion did not consist in certain religious ideas or ethical principles, but rested in the memory of historical experience. . . . She believed that Yahweh, her God, had by his mighty acts rescued her from Egypt and, *in covenant*, had made her his people.

William Dumbrell notes:

Through [God's] covenant with Israel, . . . God's concern for the whole world was expressed. [Israel was to have a mission as] the Israel of God. . . . [This] covenant relationship formed the basis of Israel's ethic. . . . Israel was called upon to demonstrate her response to the grace of her Exodus redemption by freely conforming to the covenant expectations.

Commenting on humanity generally, Dumbrell states that "human-kind stands with a more generalized covenant relationship, that which was instituted by creation itself, and implicit within this relationship is a morality which may be expected to demonstrate it."

God's acts of rescue and initiating a covenant create the basis for a Christian vision of an ethical, others-oriented life. They become our story: context, meaning, purpose and fundamental orientation. God and others are first, not me.

There are three biblical motifs that provide for me an others-first way of life:

- *The covenant with Adam and Eve (Genesis 1–2).* Adam and Eve were created to be God's first cooperative friends. Unfortunately, they are best known for their failure, which is regrettable because we then miss the real beginning of the story: God's intention for humanity.

- *The covenant with Israel (Genesis 12:1-3).* Israel is chosen by God for
  a purpose: to be his special, sent people. They are a missionary
  people embodying God's agenda and expressing, announcing, and
  demonstrating the will of God among all others: the nations, the
  Gentiles.

- *The covenant with the church (Luke 24:49; Acts 2).* Through the new
  covenant with the church humans can receive God's special blessing and be a blessing for others, and find their rightful place as
  God's renewed humanity by following the example of Jesus who
  modeled the life of working with God for the sake of others.

Putting these three covenantal thoughts together, we see that forgiveness, or being returned to covenantal faithfulness, is not the finish
line; *it's the starting line!* It is the gateway to eternal life, life derived
from and lived in the kingdom of God—for the sake of others.

THE SACRED ORDER OF THE TOWEL

I learned how being others-centered can come to fruition in a coffee
shop. Coffee shops were my offices in the late 1990s. That's where
young people wanted to meet, and it was convenient for me since
there was one right across the street from my office. I met regularly
with one or two people for spiritual direction, or groups of people
for Bible study. Because they were angry with the church and unsure
about God, it goes without saying they were also struggling with normal youthful sin: drug and alcohol abuse, and recreational sex.

As I advised them on sexuality and substance abuse, I could see that
I was getting nowhere. All I got were blank stares or counterargu-
ments that equaled or trumped my logic. In the middle of one conversation, I had a moment of enlightenment. I pictured the Upper Room
scene of John 13 where Jesus took off his robe, put a towel around his
waist and washed the disciples' feet.

At that point I said to the young couple across from me, "These moral abstractions aren't doing you any good. And now I can see that they are completely inadequate to form moral purpose and an ethical imagination that guides your daily life." They nodded in agreement. Then, I said, "Perhaps you need to answer a prior and more substantive question: fundamentally, what kind of people do you want to be?" I continued, "Do you want to be fundamentally selfish, filling your hands with drug paraphernalia and the sexual body parts of others, or do you want to fill your hands with the towel of Jesus and join with him in washing the feet of people on earth?" Going for a decision then and there I asked, "You have to choose; you can't fill your hands with both things. Only one will fit. Which will it be?"

To my pleasure and astonishment, they got it. Their lives actually changed that day as they decided to follow Jesus into what we later called "the Sacred Order of the Towel." It isn't a real order; it's just our in-house, shorthand way of reminding ourselves of the origin of Christian ethics: responding, in the manner of Jesus, to the expectations of God's covenant with humanity.

Over the next months I told them of a few spiritual disciplines I practice to keep myself focused on the incredible journey of life for the sake of others. First, I recounted a brief "vision" I had one day. I saw Jesus going about his workday humming the tune to "What a Friend I Have in Jesus." But the lyrics going through his head were: "What a friend I have in Todd; he helps me bear with the places of pain and injustice in the world; he'll be my voice when necessary, he'll do and say as I do." I told them the thought of being the friend of Jesus wasn't original to me, but it helped me imagine a moral life rooted in positive love rather than unenthusiastic prohibitions.

Second, I told them I try to be oriented to others by staying present to the moments, the events and the people I encounter each day. I do this through little prayers before the activities of each day. If I am about to speak to someone, I might whisper a little prayer like: "Jesus, make me present to this person, present to you and available to be used by you." If I am meeting someone for coffee, I might pray, "Lord, let me be your instrument of grace and peace."

Third, I told them about a prized possession that shapes my moral imagination. I am not much into "things," and I don't have any collectables, but I have a favorite ball cap that has FDNY (Fire Department of New York) on the front. But a while back, my dog chewed that cap into uselessness. Fortunately, I go to New York several times a year, so on a recent trip I tried to buy a new cap, but it being winter all I could get was a beanie, which I wear in the cold when I walk the dog, who ate my cap! (There is something wrong with this picture.) I keep the beanie as a reminder of the kind of person I wish to be. I know 9/11 illustrations are a little dicey, and I know that many years down the road some have tired of them, but this is crucial to my story, so I'm going to recount it.

I will never forget the television pictures displaying the terror of September 11, 2001. Remember the pictures of streets crowded with ash-covered people? They were doing the normal and right thing—running for their lives! Soon though, in the midst of all the replays, we all noticed movement in the opposite direction. The firefighters and other first responders were running toward the danger. The "Stay Back 200 Feet" on the back of fire trucks (and on the back of my cap) applies to others who might get in the firefighters' way as they rush into every kind of earthly hell. The men and women who are the "first responders" in our society know how to live "out of control"—meaning they have given up self-centered control for the sake of others. I haven't always known how to be out of control with the focused but seemingly unworried concentration of a firefighter. They are fine models of the Firefighter, who, knowing that he was safe in the kingdom and in the will of his Father, let the forces of this world do their worst to him.

To realize this dream of being an others-centered person, I am routinely taking opportunities to submit to God's leading in my surroundings, to be more "out of control" than I am comfortable with, to submit to my surroundings and to choose not having my own way.* I practice this so that when the events of my life unfold, I can naturally and easily embody alignment with God's story.

THE POWER OF THE HOLY

Practicing creative goodness for the sake of others may sound difficult—and naive or idealistic. I can see why. We need to keep it simple and attached to our actual life. We can't let it become a new source of busyness or produce a fresh ton of guilt. It can be a life-lifting journey. But here is a reality check: As soon as we start cooperating as a friend of Jesus, seeking to be creatively good for the sake of others, we'll realize that we can't do it on our own.

This was true for me and for thousands of others I have interacted with. I quickly saw that I needed the presence and power of the Holy Spirit to work through me. We need the Spirit's leadership, gifts and character.

FOR REFLECTION AND DISCUSSION

1. Does being others-centered deserve to be at the center of what it means to be a Christian? Why or why not?

   Can you connect the dots in your mind from Jesus as a model to your actual life?

2. Jesus obviously didn't perform miracles to show off. Why then did he do them?

---

*When I discuss submission of this type, I do not have in mind situations of abuse or illegal behavior being done to others, but the usual routines of "normal" life. The key here is that submission requires discernment in order to know what to submit to and what to get help for. A trusted friend, pastor or therapist might be needed to help us come to a healthy decision regarding possible situations of abuse.

3. What in Colossians 4:5-6 (see p. 114) grabs your imagination for serving others? Why?

4. Do you find "the Sacred Order of the Towel" useful? In what way(s)?

THROUGH THE POWER
OF THE HOLY SPIRIT

No Big Hair, No Bizarre Behavior,
Just Power for a Purpose

But you, dear friends, carefully build yourselves up in this
most holy faith by praying in the Holy Spirit,
staying right at the center of God's love, keeping your arms
open and outstretched, ready for the mercy of our Master, Jesus Christ.
This is the unending life, the real life!

JUDE 20-21

I have a mixed history regarding the person and work of the Holy Spirit. The Methodist church I was raised in certainly didn't talk about him (at least, not that I remember). Well, that is until a youth pastor invited a young evangelist from Calvary Chapel to come to our youth group. That meeting caused such a stir that the youth pastor decided to leave the Methodist church and work with Chuck Smith in Costa Mesa, California.

A few years later I came to faith, and having grown up in neighboring Santa Ana, I attended Calvary Chapel, Costa Mesa. At the time the Chapel had what they called "after glows" on Sunday nights and "Believers Meetings" on Thursdays. These were the times when church members were given the opportunity to receive Spirit in-fillings and gifts. They scared me a little bit.

Later, in Vineyard churches we experienced quite a range of Spirit activity—much of it beautiful, powerful and healing. Some of it was, well, just weird. That scared me too. But know what? When we deal with the Holy Sprit we are dealing with God! If appearances of angels scared people in the Bible, genuine connection with almighty God should be a little unnerving for us. And we don't have the luxury of ignoring the Holy Spirit. Rather we must build each other up in the Spirit, seeking to be continually filled by him and seek his presence, character and gifts.

Because I know my experience of the Spirit to be very common, I want to highlight the importance of the Holy Spirit for a life of creative cooperation with God for the sake of others. A story from a small group trying to interact with the Spirit may help. My friends e-mailed me this story because they thought it was a good example of the practices I suggest for Three Is Enough groups (see chap. 10). This is what they told me.

> Prompted by the need to provide a Christian small group to our pre-high school teens, and having just attended an Alpha conference, we decided to put together a home-based Youth Alpha. Admittedly, the two of us were very good following a recipe, but somehow we had missed creativity when the gifts were handed out. It's hard to explain, but we knew whatever was missing would be filled in by the Holy Spirit as we went along. Once we set our hands to the task, we were overwhelmed with knowing that this was God's work and we felt extreme privilege to be along for the ride.

We worked diligently to prepare by reviewing the Youth Alpha materials available, being blessed by insights, advice and stories from others already working with young teens. The Holy Spirit provided his creativity in amazing ways. Our part was simply to be available. We were anxious to put our hand to this work each week—it was more like the love of a favorite hobby and did not feel like effort. His burden is light.

The program, led by the Spirit, was creative, with video clips and different guest speakers each week to hold the kids' interest. Partnering with the Holy Spirit, we were able to dispense with our normally rigid and "by the book" styles, and expected something unexpected to happen each week. When it did, when the Spirit provided, it was always better than what we had planned: A last-minute speaker change that completely blessed the kids, an ice-breaker game to fill in time for a video glitch that was an instant hit, staffing changes for the weekend away that brought a message and the presence of the Holy Spirit in a fresh way.

As we reflect on this journey, we realize how sweetly the Holy Spirit worked inside of us, strengthening our trust in him. We were encouraged each time he stepped in to smooth the path when trouble came. And we found that the Holy Spirit enabled us to better relate to other people. The outward journey was enabled by that internal growth of compassion. The journey to follow Christ in our outward lives allows the Holy Spirit to continue to grow us inside. It is a journey of adventure and joy.

SPIRIT POWER WILL BECOME OBVIOUS

As soon as you try living a life of creative goodness on behalf of others you will see that you do not have what it takes to accomplish that dream. The Holy Spirit is the animating, energizing power for a life of cooperating with God.[†] He brings us to life; he makes the impossible possible. His power working in us makes our lives both dynamically effective and peacefully relaxed. Working alongside the Spirit, there is never a reason for us to panic, freak out or take things into our own hands.

The Holy Spirit empowers us for a purpose. While we personally experience empowerment, its effects are directed toward others. The Spirit enables us to embody the kingdom story as God's ambassadors. The gifts of the Spirit, for instance, are simply tools that enable us to serve the people we encounter in our everyday life. The fruit of the Spirit is the character he produces in us. I'm quite sure that God works his character into our life for more reasons than I know, but I'm sure one reason is that we need his character in order to work well with his power.

The familiar saying "power corrupts" generally seems true to me. The Spirit, however, works in us in two ways: giving (1) power, and (2) the ethics, character and morals of the kingdom to go along with it. In my own imagination, I've always used the picture Paul paints of Jesus in Philippians 2:5-8 as my model for the kind of character the Spirit wants to work in me along with the power of the Spirit.

SPIRIT POWER IS CONTROVERSIAL

As we begin to think about the person and role of the Holy Spirit, I want to highlight a fascinating but sad reality. I am aware that in many parts of the church the Holy Spirit is more of a controversy than a comfort. However, even if we believed that the spiritual gifts of Romans 12, 1 Corinthians 12 and Ephesians 4 do not apply to us, we are still left to answer two questions: Why, according to John 13–17, were the first disciples so angst-filled at the thought of Jesus leaving them? How was the sending of the Holy Spirit the prescription for their emotional ailment?

[†]See appendix 2 for a brief introduction to the person and work of the Holy Spirit.

I suggest this answer: Jesus was humanity and Israel as God intended them; he was the perfect covenantal-kingdom partner. He did life right! And the disciples knew this. As Peter observed, "Master, to whom would we go? You have the words of real life, eternal life" (John 6:68). So as Jesus was preparing to leave earth, he promised not to leave the disciples orphaned but to send the Holy Spirit—another Comforter—so that they (and we) would have the desire and the capacity to live as Jesus did, as the cooperative friends of God, creatively doing good for the sake of others—through the power of the Holy Spirit.

Jesus told his first followers to not go out on their own to minister in his name until they had received the empowering of the Holy Spirit, who came at Pentecost (Luke 24:49). The Spirit is the continuing presence of Jesus. He gives the character (fruit), gifts, power and authority to be Jesus' cooperative friends. How then has the Spirit become controversial? What happened? What has caused such skittishness about his presence and his work?

Having spent a great deal of time around classical Pentecostals, charismatics and third-wavers,[‡] I have seen every excess imaginable. I empathize with those looking for a sane way to relate to the Spirit. But whatever our past experience, whatever previous views we have been taught, one thing is clear: Christianity without the manifest presence of the Spirit is subbiblical. It is not enough to criticize what has been wrong in the past. To be Jesus' cooperative friends, we must build a positive, constructive way of life that is animated, energized and

---

[‡]Peter Wagner, professor of evangelism and church growth at Fuller Seminary, coined this term in the mid- to late-1980s. In Wagner's words, the first wave of the Spirit in the twentieth century came at the turn of the century—somewhere around 1901. The second happened among mainline churches and Catholics in the late 1970s. By "the third wave," Wagner meant mostly mainstream evangelicals who were experiencing Spirit phenomena but not using classic Pentecostal theology to explain the experiences.

guided by the power of the Holy Spirit.

All Christians agree that Jesus is the head of the church and that the Holy Spirit is the continuing presence of Christ in the church. We need to move, however, from theological lip service to action by repenting of grieving the Holy Spirit, which we do by ignoring or distrusting him, *and* by attributing bizarre behaviors to him.

It is crucial that we invite the Spirit into our communities of faith and that we prayerfully listen to him. Through this we will develop a conversational relationship with God similar to the relationships we see in Scripture. As we live in creative goodness, we will, like children learning to walk or speak, take appropriate risks, in faith, knowing that our Father will be beside us. Experiential religion is the biblical norm and the only kind of religion that will be attractive in a contemporary culture.

The Holy Spirit's power is given for a purpose. In my vision, I see the cooperative friends of Jesus arising every day knowing that for the sake of serving others God could work any gift of the Spirit through them at any given moment.

I imagine that what I've just said makes some people nervous. Some may be cynical, and still others may be thinking, *Been there, done that. Got the scars and T-shirts to prove it!* If you are one of these, I've got an important and hope-filled response: It's true, you are right, this Holy Spirit journey can be nutty stuff, but *the answer to misuse is not no use, it is right use.*

I've pretty much seen and heard it all over the years. I've experienced enough to make "the good, the bad and the ugly" look downright plain. Whether you've walked a similar road or this whole Holy Spirit discussion is new to you, I have a few observations for developing a constructive interface with the Holy Spirit, an engagement that others will experience as for their good rather than the source of religious jokes.

GOD WORKS THROUGH YOU

The gifts of the Spirit listed in the New Testament are not to be understood as being constantly possessed by any given believer. I think it is best to view the gifts as owned by God and dispensed as he sees fit (1 Corinthians 12:7-11), depending on the occasion. This view helps us resolve the apparent contrast in Paul's statement that not everyone has such-and-such a gift with his encouragement to "eagerly desire the greater gifts." According to Pentecostal scholar Gordon Fee the "greater gifts" Paul mentions in 1 Corinthians 12:31 does not mean more important gifts but those that have superior intelligibility in the community. Fee emphasizes that the gifts build up Christians for serving each other and the world.

It is true, however, that God so routinely blesses certain people with a gift, say teaching, that they can say, "I have the gift of teaching." This is experientially true to me. When I stand up to teach I don't find myself thinking, *Gee, I wonder if I will get the gift of teaching tonight?* Similarly, in situations where I am the acknowledged leader, I don't wonder if the gift of leadership will come. On the other hand, when I am called to a hospital to pray for the sick, I usually ask for the gift of healing because I am not regularly gifted in healing.

Here's the takeaway—even if you're a little skittish about the gifts of the Spirit—the cooperative friends of Jesus need the enabling of God's Spirit to serve others. We simply can't retreat from this biblical truth. Here's a safe way to start: No matter what you think about the spiritual gifts, believe that the Holy Spirit can use you in surprising and unexpected ways that bring joy to you and others.

BE NATURALLY SUPERNATURAL

When interacting with the Holy Spirit, don't do anything manipulative or for effect. We can partner with the Holy Spirit in normal ways. For instance, when we discern that the Holy Spirit is nudging us to say something—what the Bible might call a word of knowledge, wisdom, discernment or prophecy—we don't need to use an authoritative tone of voice, stand on a table or shout. It's possible, and appropriately humble, to say in an everyday conversational tone:

> You know, (insert a friend's name here), I might be crazy or eating food that doesn't agree with me, but I've really had you on my mind a lot the last few days. I'm sensing that you might be feeling some unusual confusion about what to do with your life. I'm not sure, but this morning when I was praying for you I felt like the Spirit spoke to me and told me to tell you the silence does not mean that God doesn't care about your confusion and fear. In fact, the impression I was getting is that God is really pleased with your desire to hear him and that the answer will come soon.

We can say this in a natural manner with an unassuming, non-religious attitude. When we do, several good things happen. Those receiving our words are left in control of their life before God. That is huge. Life in the Spirit has no place for dishonest manipulation or an attitude that draws attention to us.

DON'T MAKE THIS JOURNEY ALL ABOUT CHURCH MEETINGS

As we explore a new way to be Christian, our actual life is always in view. This is especially true regarding our relationship with the Holy Spirit. Though they may not mean to, I've noticed that many churches give the unintended message that "ministry time" happens in the front of the church sanctuary or meeting room. Ministry obviously does happen up front in worship, but it is not limited to there. Many Christians have the wrong impression that the only place where "the anointing comes" or "the Spirit really moves" is near the church altar when especially gifted people are leading. This is a real loss for the kingdom.

The kingdom is a secular and public reality. This may sound subversive or counterintuitive, but it is true. *Secular* simply means "of the world" or "in solidarity with the world," which the rule and reign of God surely is. As Ray Anderson helpfully puts it:

> The Gospel of the kingdom of God as announced by John and pronounced through the ministry of Jesus restored the workplace of human life under the reign of God's kingdom to be authentically human and deeply spiritual as a secular sacrament. . . .
>
> From the perspective of the kingdom of God, there is only one workplace. It is where humans live as material and spiritual beings.
>
> [Jesus] called [us] to work out [our] salvation for the sake of the kingdom of God in [our] own workplace. His gospel was a gospel of the kingdom of God, not the church. . . . He did not come to build a kingdom here on earth, but to empower others to kingdom living. While the church tends to differentiate itself from the world by its religious nature, the kingdom of God penetrates and transforms the world by its secular nature.

The gifts of the Holy Spirit only work well when they are exercised in *all* of the places God works—mainly in "the world." I'm not slamming the church. But one hour a week in the church building does not come close to the 167 hours lived outside of those walls. If God worked only within the walls of our church plants, he'd be bored. He works in the world, with all people and all the affairs of humankind. In this sense, the church is a part of the world too.

God loves the world and is in solidarity with it. As we cooperate with him in being creatively good for the sake of others, we'll discover we're on the most exciting journey in the Holy Spirit we can imagine.

God is at work in church buildings too. There, I find plenty of opportunities to be an ambassador of the kingdom. I've experienced the outer journey (others-oriented) and the inner journey (spiritual transformation) in the routines of my professional religious life. You can too—in church and wherever else you spend your waking hours.

EMPOWERED BUT NOT IN CONTROL

Growth in the Spirit does not lead to control. While on earth Jesus respected the choices of those he encountered. He let the rich young ruler walk away. He let Judas betray him. We must operate with the same respect for the freedom God gives humans. Bad things happen when we try to use our gifts to manipulate others—even when we think the Spirit is guiding us. The will to "win" normally leads to harming others. This is never from the Holy Spirit.

We can't control life in the Spirit; it's contrary to being the servants of Jesus. In the kingdom we are God's ambassadors. Ambassadors live with two seemingly contradictory realities. On the one hand an ambassador is the highest ranking representative of his or her country in the nation he or she is placed. On the other hand, the ambassador can do nothing of his or her own will. Ambassadors simply carry out the will of their government in the place they were sent to serve. That's us. We are God's ambassadors on earth to carry out his will through the power of the Holy Spirit.

One more thing: some Christians have misused the notion of *faith*. From the Gospel accounts it's clear that faith in the work of God is very important. Jesus routinely notices and praises people for their faith. And Jesus never says, "By your cynicism or appropriate skepticism you are healed." Nevertheless, our faith never controls God. We cannot by our faith force God to do what we want, when we want it. Nevertheless, sincere, hope-filled, risk-taking, Spirit-empowered and Spirit-controlled faith is required to be the cooperative friends of Jesus.

DIAL DOWN EMOTIONS

Dialing down human emotion is not a denial or denigration of emotion. But sometimes, what is going on inside us hinders clear discernment of the movement of the Holy Spirit. I'm not suggesting we set aside an essential part of our humanness, only that we should dial down enough to be present and alert to the wind of the Spirit. The following stories illustrate this reality.

> By now [Jesus and the apostles] had arrived at the house of the town official, and pushed their way through the gossips looking for a story and the neighbors bringing in casseroles. Jesus was abrupt: "Clear out! This girl isn't dead. She's sleeping." They told him he didn't know what he was talking about. But when Jesus had gotten rid of the crowd, he went in, took the girl's hand, and pulled her to her feet—alive. The news was soon out, and traveled throughout the region. (Matthew 9:23-26)

> Some of the disciples had heard that Peter was visiting in nearby Lydda and sent two men to ask if he would be so kind as to come over. Peter got right up and went with them. They took him into the room where Tabitha's body was laid out. Her old friends, most of them widows, were in the room mourning. They showed Peter pieces of clothing the Gazelle had made while she was with them. Peter put the widows all out of the room. He knelt and prayed. Then he spoke directly to the body: "Tabitha, get up."
> She opened her eyes. When she saw Peter, she sat up. He took her hand and helped her up. Then he called in the believers and widows, and presented her to them alive. (Acts 9:38-41)

Thinking of these passages, have you ever wondered why both Jesus and Peter asked the people in the room to leave before they resuscitated these two? The texts don't say, so we have to read between the lines. My best guess is that Jesus and Peter knew there was a big difference between faith and the emotions felt by the family and friends of sick people. Emotions, while totally fine and normal, are not the same as faith. Getting all worked up neither moves God nor changes molecules. Emotions are simply the spontaneous and involuntary feelings we experience throughout life, and having them is fine. But the kinds of emotions going on around Jesus and Peter weren't helpful or faith-filled, and they did not facilitate healing.

On a recent spring break, my wife, daughter and I took a driving vacation through the central and northern coast of California. If you've been there, you know it is notoriously foggy. Driving along hilly country roads, I found it unnerving to crest a hill to see nothing! Just a sheet of whiteness! Yet a few seconds later we could be in another microclimate where the air was crystal clear. While cooperating with Jesus through the movements and rhythms of the Holy Spirit, unchecked emotions create a blinding fog. Attentiveness to the Spirit creates blue-sky discernment. As we learn through experience and become skilled at working with the Holy Spirit, we will occasionally fall down. No worries. The first followers of Jesus fell down. Everyone since has too. We are on a learning curve. It's important that we pay attention: to ourselves, to others and to the Holy Spirit. Be aware of the first two, but *follow* the latter. Dialing down emotions and tuning in to the Spirit is basic training for cooperative friends of Jesus.

POSITIVE ALTERNATIVES

Here is some happy news: you can't fail by trying. We are on a lifelong learning curve, which may even last into the life to come. So just go for it. When you do, you'll have at least a few successes, and likely more. People, who under normal circumstances would continue to suffer, will be healed and helped when you step out in faith. Under God's tutelage, if you are humble and honest, you will experience personal growth in the things of the Spirit—things that manifest God's kingdom for the benefit others. As you step out, you can expect the following:

- *A new sense of power and authority.* This does not need to make us into arrogant celebrities. Power is simply ability, capacity or the means necessary to carry out our vocation as the cooperative friends of Jesus. Authority is the divine authorization or endorsement to do so. There is nothing here for us to get a big head over—it's all God, sheer grace.

• *Divine appointments.* As we become alert to the movements of the Holy Spirit, we will become simultaneously alert to the people and events of our life and pay attention to the Holy Spirit. We will discover that God has prearranged people to meet and things to do. These divine appointments will pop up in everyday life—like a computer pop-up reminder of a meeting.

At a serendipitous time of a divine appointment, you may wonder where to start. How do you engage friends and coworkers in a way that they experience the interaction as loving and kind? Here is a simple pattern to use. It's like using training wheels—use it until it comes natural.

First, engage your counterpart in conversation; listen both to him or her and to the Holy Spirit. Be alert; pay attention. Try to understand what is happening with the person. In the first step you are trying to answer the question, *What does this person want me to pray for or do?*

Second, make a diagnosis: Step one is an interview, so to speak. Like a doctor or a therapist, you are trying, through the conversation and the leading of the Holy Spirit, to discern what is going on in the person's life. You want to answer the question, *What is happening in this situation?*

Third, decide, based on your discernment from step one, what the Spirit is leading you to do. Should you pray? Give counsel? Give a hug? Just listen? There is no pattern we can reliably follow here. Each situation is different. Just because it worked a certain way last time, doesn't mean it will be the same this time. In this phase of the conversation, try to answer the question, *How should I now respond?*

Fourth, act on God's leading: give a word of comfort or wisdom, say a prayer, lend a hand or whatever is appropriate. The question here is designed to keep the process real: *What is happening as we pray or act on behalf of this person?*

Fifth, check in with your counterpart. Ask if the person felt anything as you prayed or acted, if he or she had any insights or the like. In short, just be real, honest. Often, in this last step, God will lead you or your counterpart to further understanding or additional steps toward healing or insight. The question in this final step is, *What should this person—or both of us—do now?*

These simple steps can't be made into a formula for automatic success. They are just simple ways for beginners to get started. As you practice and grow, you may discover a pattern that works better. Hopefully following these steps will remove the fear that ministry in the Holy Spirit is weird. I recognize why reasonable people might feel this way. But Jesus said that the Holy Spirit would be the animating, empowering and character-building presence of God for the church. Wouldn't it be weird to not depend on and interact with him? We just need a model to get started. These five steps can get us going on the road to effective, straightforward and sane ministry in the Holy Spirit.

It's possible to get comfortable with the journey of discernment. Stick to the values outlined in this book and you will be fine. As long as your counterpart leaves the conversation feeling understood and loved, you have done well. That is the worst-case scenario. Best case is the thrill of watching God work through your faithful participation in divine appointments.

There is an old observation that I find helpful. What's the difference between the Dead Sea and Sea of Galilee? The Sea of Galilee flows into another body of water—the Jordan River. And that flow gives the sea and the river, and all that is in them, life. The Dead Sea, however, has no outlet, no place to go. Thus it is, well, dead.

Life in the Spirit is just like that. Without an outlet, without a focus on others, life in the Spirit becomes stale. It has no power to create life in others. At some point such a life actually stops being "in the Spirit" because life in the Spirit, by definition, means giving life to others.

COME HOLY SPIRIT

Seeing the essential connection between conversion and a life of service not only properly locates conversion in God's love and purposes for people, it makes sense of the continuing work of the Holy Spirit. If our concern is merely going to heaven when we die, then the person and work of the Holy Spirit will not mean much.

If, however, we see conversion in covenantal and kingdom terms, if we see that to be a follower of Jesus means to announce, demonstrate and embody the gospel of the kingdom, the need for and value of the Holy Spirit is evident. Bible scholar Gordon Smith notes that "in Acts the defining feature of conversion is the presence of the Spirit in the life of the new believer." We have drifted far from that picture of the early church. We might say the defining feature is "She believes," "He went forward," "She said the prayer," "They are sure they are going to heaven" or something similar.

There is a straightforward reason for this change of thinking. We have lost the complete story of God and instead have a story rooted in our problem (sin), our need (forgiveness), and our desire (heaven). However, when we discover God's story—a cooperative people who do creative good for the sake of others—the need for the personally experienced presence and power of the Holy Spirit comes front and center. Life energized by and animated through the power of the Spirit is attractive to today's seekers. They want to know God and his power. Mere mental assent to doctrine will never do. They want to *experience* God; indeed, all of us want to feel linked to God, merged into an alliance that results in changed life. Seekers also have a gut feeling that a relationship with God should be experienced as good by those in their social circles and by the hurting and the oppressed.

Through God's full story, seekers will know they have indeed found and connected to God.

The person and work of the Holy Spirit has another important practical application for contemporary seekers. They often prefer to learn new truths experientially. This is how they know something is real. It is common today to hear that someone came to faith because he or she sensed the presence of God, witnessed the healing of a friend or was touched by God in some way. When the work of the Spirit is active in a community of faith, seekers hear a language they understand and value.

I have put forward a simple way to understand God's story: (1) cooperative friends, (2) creative goodness, (3) for others, (4) the power of the Holy Spirit. Now, I'd like us to think about how we might tell this story to those who don't know it.

FOR REFLECTION AND DISCUSSION

1. List three or four ways you can "build yourself up in the Holy Spirit."

2. What do you think of the idea that, in addition to the common ways God uses you, he can, as the situation requires, give you any spiritual gift?

3. What do you think of the few values—be natural, don't confine the Spirit to church, yield control to the Spirit, and dial down emotions—laid out for interacting with the Holy Spirit?

   What would you add to this list?

4. What has been your predominant experience with the Holy Spirit (excess, ignoring him, something healthy/just about right)?

5. Can you pray with faith and anticipation, "Come Holy Spirit"? Why or why not?

INVITING OTHERS TO

LIVE A NEW WAY

A Fresh Approach to Sharing Our Faith

"I've got a surprise for you," I said to the young man who had come to see me. His dad and I have been friends since before either of us had children. I'd known "Tommy" since he was in diapers. In junior high school Tommy, bored with the church meetings his parents found so refreshing and life-changing, began to think, *Maybe religion isn't for me.* He wondered why—no, he was hurt by why—he didn't feel God the way his parents and their friends did. Other kids at church and school came to faith. Tommy hurt; he figured God didn't like him or want him. *You ignore me,* he thought, *so I'll ignore you too.*

Tommy's attitude toward God lasted until his senior year of college. Several things were rumbling around in his mind during the first semester of what he knew would be a pivotal year. First, he had studied accounting but was unsure he could live his whole life immersed in the world of numbers. He discovered in some of his other business classes that he liked the people part of business. He enjoyed his management, marketing and human-resources classes. Having never questioned his pursuit of a career as an auditor, Tommy was shaken. He was mentally and emotionally exhausted from fighting off the fear that he had wasted several years and sixty thousand dollars. What did it all mean?

In the midst of this serious introspection, Tommy's best friend from high school, attending an out-of-state college, contracted cancer around his spine. The ensuing operation to remove the tumor caused his friend to lose use of most of his body. Tommy felt guilty that he was not able to be with his friend in this time of need. Now, he began to feel that he was "slipping." He knew he was not himself. Tracey, Tommy's girlfriend, knew it too.

Tracey lived her whole life with a depressed dad whose medication, when he took it, made him distant and blank. But without the meds he was impossible to live with. When he was home, Mom and the kids avoided him by hiding in some part of the house. Tracey took one look into Tommy's sullen, empty eyes and immediately knew where this was going. She also knew where she was going—out of the relationship. She was looking for a place to run, a way to escape the pain and fear that raced around her nervous system at the sight of depression in someone she loved.

That was too much loss for Tommy. He began to doubt most everything in life, but mostly himself. He was looking for a way to be grounded, to be "normal," as he put it to me.

This search led him to start reading spiritual material. His newly found fascination with and love of people had led him to the idea that there was "reality" in the unseen world. For instance, he realized that though he couldn't see the oncovirus that attacked his friend's spine, he could see the effect. Neither could he see the power that grounded his parents in love for God and others, but he could see its effect. He couldn't see his changing passions, but he knew they were real. Mostly, he couldn't see inside Tracey, but he could feel the pain of her rejection.

Tommy came to me with a clear agenda, which he told me of before he came. He said he trusted me to tell him the truth—"No baloney." He wanted to know what it means to be a Christian. He wanted assurance that it could make a difference in his actual life. He wanted to know if there was something there, invisible but real, that would manifest itself in his life.

After his fairly intense story and the follow-up questions, the room fell silent. Tommy seemed to exert significant energy in order to drag his eyes off the floor to meet mine. Without words, he seemed to implore me, "Okay, what do you have to say to all that?"

Gathering my thoughts, I said to him, "Well, here is the surprise. I've got some compelling questions for you; inquisitive thoughts that may help you come to your own conclusions: If you knew you were going to live tomorrow, the next day and for a long, long time, who would you follow? Around what story would you organize the various parts of your life? What kind of person would you be? How would you determine the answer?"

How to Become an Apprentice of Jesus

Putting those questions to Tommy I was trying to avoid the Christian sales pitch. This is important today. Most people think they have heard the gospel and rejected it. I see a huge opportunity in this state of affairs. I want to communicate the gospel according to Jesus, the in-breaking of the kingdom of God to heal and restore the earth, and to remake humanity as God originally intended it. Life in the kingdom is the best news anyone could receive. In the New Testament those who "got" the invitation of Jesus did everything necessary to rearrange their life to follow him. Today's seekers will do the same when they hear the story about becoming followers of God in the way of Jesus.

Theology and apologetics are fine; there is a place for them. But our all-purpose explanation is genuinely embodied love. Love—being others-oriented, as I have been describing it—is the door opener. It tells others Christians are safe, that we are not trying to win, that this is not about us. Loving openness is what Tommy hoped for in our conversation.

To love is "to will the good of others," others of all kinds no matter what worldview they may hold as they are coming to faith. There is no preferable or "right" place from which to start following Jesus. All who come to him come from some difficult place where they are trapped. Such is the nature of sin. The nature of love, however, is the antidote for being trapped and enticement to a peace-filled, rescued life—human life as God intended. An evangelistic approach of love is characterized by the apostle Paul:

> Love doesn't strut,
> Doesn't have a swelled head,
> Doesn't force itself on others, . . .
> Doesn't revel when others grovel,
> Takes pleasure in the flowering of truth. (1 Corinthians 13:4-6)

Evangelistic approaches that manifest such love are not weak or reactionary. On the contrary, they come from the ultimate source of strength: God who is love.

These days most seekers aren't wondering about doctrines. In my experience, it's rare for someone to start a conversation about faith with a question about the Trinity, the atonement, the virgin birth or the resurrection. These may be real issues to seekers, but I find them leading with questions such as, Is Christianity real? Does it work for you—make a difference for you? Are you becoming a better person? Does it heal your relationships? They want to know what it is like to follow Jesus.

An author relates a beautiful little story that powerfully demonstrates that while sin, forgiveness and heaven are important to the Christian story, the story itself cannot be reduced to them. The story is about the kind of life God intends for humanity.

> One morning I went to the back door to call our three-year-old son. I planned for him to go with me to town on an errand. As I opened the back door to call, I saw him—but what a predica-

ment he was in. The little fellow had been playing in the garden and had fallen in the mud. So as I called him it was now with a two-fold purpose: there was the overshadowing purpose—taking him to town with me; but there was also the incidental need of "washing up" which must be incorporated into the purpose. I must first minister some "grace" so that my purpose could be fulfilled.

I think this story uses grace in too narrow a way. The whole deal is grace: going to the door, calling, planning, purpose, washing and fulfillment. Nevertheless, the larger point shines through. Our new life in the kingdom involves doing some really cool stuff with "Dad."

Because we have all sinned—played in the garden and fallen in the mud—entering a new kind of life (eternal life) includes repentance and forgiveness, a reordering, refocusing and redirection of our life. God's forgiveness is obviously the free gift of God in Christ. Nothing we do in response gains favor with God; it doesn't earn forgiveness. But I believe that our sincere effort to recalibrate our life around his purposes pleases him. There is no greater joy in my life than seeing my children taking on godly values in imitation of their mother or me, as imperfect as we are. (In fact, I'm thrilled when they take out the trash or empty the dishwasher without being reminded!)

Think then about the satisfaction God must feel when we turn to him and imitate his Son. Repenting (turning back) reconciles the broken relationship we have with God, and the Holy Spirit regenerates us, remaking us into the humans God intended. But—and this is crucial for both evangelism and discipleship—repentance, forgiveness and regeneration and are not ends unto themselves. Yes, through them we are certain of entering heaven, but we also have a new kind of life. Like Jesus, we live for the sake of others. We become cooperative friends of God, creatively doing good for others through the power, character and gifts of the Holy Spirit.

This perspective makes sense to present-day seekers. It often sounds to them like an alternative version of the Christian story. Actually, it's the only story, the original story. And when it is recounted in this manner, people are willing to listen. It's a window through which they sneak a peek at true Christianity, and they find they're attracted to it.

Seekers intuitively know that there must be something more to being a Christian than adherence to abstract theological data. They just don't know what it could be. But they get excited by lives that transcend fame, power or wealth through serving others. This is why so many people—Christians and non-Christians alike—are fascinated by Oprah, Bono and Mother Teresa. The church should take note. Here is a wide open door. Let's tell the story of the cooperative friends of God who creatively serve others.

BROOKS AND DUNN ON CHRISTIANITY

When it comes to popular culture, especially TV, movies and music, I am so uncool I could be a minor heat wave. I'm neither bragging nor knocking it, I am just way too busy to watch TV or keep up with current music. My wife and kids get it though—they're cool. They try their best to keep me hip, but it is a nearly impossible task. Not long ago, my wife, who likes country music, took me to a concert in which the famous country duo Brooks and Dunn were the headliners. A couple of groups opened for them, and I thought they were really good. They were obviously professional in every sense of the word—tight musically with great vocals. But when Brooks and Dunn came out, it was clear they were in a different class. They were a stage show; the others, simply bands. The whole arena leaped to their feet at first sight of the duo, and danced and bounced with the music for the remainder of the evening. The place was electric, and it was clear the crowd felt a personal connection with Brooks and Dunn, with the stage elements, and with the music.

The arena was buzzing, and it was hard to imagine there could be any kind of crescendo or climax to the night. But, being the country music novice I am, I didn't know Brooks and Dunn had one more big song up their sleeve, their hit "Only in America."

As Brooks and Dunn performed this song, thousands of streamers and a storm of red, white and blue confetti began to fall on us all. Just then, with no hint of what was to come, three amazing looking—iconic, really—young Marines walked on stage, marching in stereotypical military correctness. Arriving at the center of the stage, they turned crisply to face the audience. The dress blues of the Marine Corp is the only U.S. military uniform composed of the three colors of the U.S. flag. They were truly stunning in their ink-blue uniforms trimmed by the famous blood-red stripe that honors their fallen comrades. Golden buttons gleamed in the bright stage lights and their white hats glowed like a halo. As they stood at attention, blankly gazing toward the audience, the crowd erupted into the loudest applause, whistling and cheering I have ever heard—ten times louder than their response to the bands.

I am not overstating this. I've been to hundreds of professional baseball, football, basketball and hockey games. But I've never heard such a roar as when the Marines appeared. As a keen observer of people, I stood there thinking, *What's happening here?* Clearly some of it was the mix of beer, patriotism and the hype of a concert. But there was something more. People deeply respect and are moved by sacrifice for the sake of others (even sacrifice that allows everyone in America a chance to dream and dance). It pulls on our hearts. In it, I believe, echoes God's pre-creation intention. Sacrifice in the service of others is at the heart of what it means to human, to bear the image of God. I'm not suggesting that the Brooks and Dunn fans were celebrating all this, only that being a truly good person, someone who sacrifices for others, is powerfully attractive and a wonderful apologetic. I don't know of anything else that can more easily open doors to explain the Christian faith.

ISN'T THIS WORKS?

Some Christians might be uncomfortable with what I am saying. They may be afraid that in minimizing belief and emphasizing action that I am failing to draw a clear line between true evangelism and the Social Gospel, between who is truly Christian and who isn't. I'm not trying to be controversial; I'm trying to help. Hang in there with me and maybe you will agree that life rooted in belief is better than naked belief.

A preoccupation with who is "in" and who is "out," and how we differentiate between the two, has dominated Christian thinking for about five hundred years. This is somewhat of an oversimplification; when we think of being "in" we hardly think about "what" we are in *to*. Normally we are concerned with how to get in. Even if we say someone gets in by faith alone, which I believe is correct, we're still left with the question, How do we know who has faith and is justified?

So that people would not be perpetually accused by their conscience or manipulated by the church, many Christian leaders from the Reformation forward have, from a sincere desire to help, tried to give assurance of salvation on the basis of a lowest common denominator. It has been thought that the best benchmark is to have a minimum set of required beliefs. Just give mental assent to certain doctrines and you are in. Behavior—actually following Jesus—has been seen as an aside. Good to get to if you can but not essential. The problem with behavior is it gets too slippery. After all, everyone misbehaves now and then—but they usually do so with their beliefs intact—which keeps them "in."*

Some Christian leaders worry that focusing on character transformation, spiritual formation, personal piety or self-sacrifice will result

---

*I know that in many traditions, once you are "in," behaviors do come into play— sometimes in very legalistic ways. But in my experience, the line marking "in" from "out" was painted with minimalist beliefs, not behaviors associated with following Jesus for the sake of others.

in navel gazing, narcissistic introspection or self-righteousness. Some Protestants have told me they think that these practices sound "Catholic," as if following Jesus is somehow "works," while what Protestants care about is grace. We fear that if we do anything, we are somehow robbing God of glory. Dallas Willard effectively counters this notion:

> Those who think that the cultivation of inner Christ-likeness through personal discipleship to Jesus amounts to a "privatization" of our faith in him ("quietism" and "pietism" are words often used in that connection) simply do not understand how the spiritual life in Christ works. You *cannot* privatize the fire of God that burns through the life of a disciple of Jesus. This was Jesus' point in saying that "a city built on a hill cannot be hid."

Our culture cries out for such light. Most people know our world is walking in significant moral darkness and ethical confusion. Sex, medicine, nation-states, politics, education, corporations, poverty, world religions, terrorism, bioethics—nothing seems to be ethically rooted these days. We have access to more information than any previous generation, but it doesn't seem to be making us wiser, better people. To quote an old lyric from Larry Norman, "Sometimes I think we've advanced, but then I look at where we are."

I predict that a revival of actual Christian living—of people living truly good, others-oriented lives—will be to twenty-first-century evangelism what mass evangelism and seeker churches were to the twentieth. Genuinely good people who can humbly tell the Christian story in everyday conversations will be cherished guides for those struggling toward faith in Jesus. Today's seekers are convinced not so much by information or argument as by seeing the life of God in others, that is, seeing a Christian's life spilling over to others in love, generosity and sacrifice. When I was a young evangelist, we used to say the exact opposite. "Don't look at us," we would exclaim, "We are imperfect and will let you down. Look at Jesus. He is perfect and will never let you down."

While that statement is true about humans, it doesn't change the fact that seekers today *are* looking at us. They want us to show them the way. They aren't looking for right words or the best arguments. They are looking through our eyes to the windows of our soul. When the life of God indwells us, they can see it is real and thus a possibility for them too. Seekers don't expect us to be perfect; they won't reject God because we sometimes fail. However, they will reject faith that makes no effort to cooperate with God to become truly good persons for the sake of others.

TALKING ABOUT WHAT GOD IS UP TO

Seekers wonder, what is this whole "Christian thing" supposed to mean? Not hearing an intelligent and coherent life-shaping answer in the church, only a garbled, nonsensical message, seekers often give up. Most contemporary evangelistic preaching calls seekers to receive forgiveness of sins through Jesus. The goal, of course, is to gain heaven when they die. This distorts the plan of God and the biblical data.

A better, more powerful, imagination-shaping view is that Jesus forgives us so we can experience "total life change" (Luke 24:45; Acts 13:23). God grants this real and lasting life now for a further pur-pose—to be the people of God, people specially sent to be ambassa-dors of his kingdom in their daily spheres of influence.

Prior to communicating with seekers, we should ask ourselves, *In what direction are the people around us heading? What is God doing here? What is our place in this?* Then we look for opportunities to talk about God's purposes for and love of creation and humans; how creation and humans can find healing, reconciliation and fulfillment; and where creation and humanity will end.

The Bible has a special and powerful word, *telos*, which is often translated as "end," as we commonly use the word; for example, "the end of the story" or "the end of the game." But sometimes it means much more: completion, having a purposeful order that reaches a perfect climax, a dream coming to fruition, a hope fulfilled and the like.

Giving the Christian story—following Jesus—a new *telos* will strike a chord with today's seekers. Sadly, seekers often reject the gospel, particularly when it is presented as "the ticket to heaven when you die." But their rejection of this wrongheaded message also has a golden lining. First, they have prompted the church to a fresh and more biblical telling of our story. Second, they have opened a door to engaging them on their terms, which is the best place to start a conversion. We need to grapple with their questions related to experiencing true meaning on earth. When we communicate new life in the kingdom of God with freshness, we will garner a new hearing.

INVITING OTHERS INTO A GOD-FASHIONED LIFE

You may be wondering, *What practical implications does this new way of looking at God's story have for evangelism? How do we invite others into a God-fashioned life?* Here's how it's shaped me. I invite people to experience life in Jesus. I don't deny the importance of sin or wrath or heaven or hell. I simply announce the good news of the in-breaking of God's kingdom through the person and work of Jesus. I tell them they can be in on it if they so choose.

If they reject the good news, I find that bringing up God's wrath rarely changes their mind. Anybody who has raised children or even babysat for a few minutes knows this is true. When people are intent on doing something, threats of future consequences does little to change their minds. (The failure of capital punishment to prevent murder is a case in point!) The realignment in view here must come from an inner motivation lit on fire by God himself. My job is to accurately and winsomely tell the story. If a fire is lit and the seeker begins to follow, God will certainly deal with his or her sin—both revealing it and forgiving it through Christ.

Knowing that Tommy had rejected the faith, I reached across my

desk to grab a note pad. Over the next ten or fifteen minutes, wanting Tommy to not only grasp what I was saying but to be able to retell
the story to others as well, I unpacked the four phrases I have used
throughout this book (see the following diagrams).

I began, "Tommy, being a Christian means to be . . ."

The cooperative friend of Jesus. It means that you see the story
of your life within the story of God—within his intention for
humanity. As soon as you attempt that, you will see your sin;
you will see where and how you have chosen your own path,
written your own story. When sin becomes clear, so will the
life, sacrificial death and resurrection of Jesus, and the eternal
life in the kingdom it brings. Through faith, trust and confidence in Christ you will find both forgiveness and the gift of
reorienting your life. This is known as repentance. It's a lifestyle
in which we enter a new life in the kingdom of God—with
heaven to come.

Seeking to live consistent lives of creative goodness. God is up to
something; he is healing and restoring his creation. His chosen
agents for this creative activity are those who want in on this
divine conspiracy to overcome evil with good.

For the sake of others. In God's name, and according to his plan,
loving and serving others is the very heart of Christian life.[†] Other
people are the endgame. Because of God's plan for them in the

---

[†]"This is my command: Love one another the way I loved you. This is the very best
way to love. Put your life on the line for your friends. You are my friends when you
do the things I command you. I'm no longer calling you servants because servants
don't understand what their master is thinking and planning. No, I've named you
friends because I've let you in on everything I've heard from the Father" (John
15:12-15).

renewed cosmos, others are where the real action is.

Through the power of the Holy Spirit. The Spirit is the Continuator. He is the continuing presence of Jesus—as Jesus promised (John 14–16). The Continuator is my favorite image of the Holy Spirit. Experientially knowing that Jesus is still present with us, in us and in the world through the person and work of the Holy Spirit animates and empowers me to seek a life of creative goodness for the sake of others.

I've thought about and used this outline for many years now. Nevertheless, I am amazed every time I use it. It astounds me that through focusing on others I find God, his forgiveness and what he is up to—and I find my truest, most human-in-the-image-of-God self.

In chapter ten we will discuss a vision for participating in groups dedicated to the journey inward and the journey outward in order to embody, announce and demonstrate the kingdom of God.

For Reflection and Discussion

1. How have you approached faith-sharing with people like Tommy? What happened? What did you learn?

2. Does the thought of inviting someone to be an apprentice of Jesus make the idea of sharing your faith easier or harder? Why?

3. Do you think the four diagrams are helpful? Why or why not?

4. Glance back at the leading, open-ended questions on page 141. Do they seem useful to you? Why or why not?

THREE IS ENOUGH GROUPS

A New Way to Live

By yourself you're unprotected.
With a friend you can face the worst.
Can you round up a third?
A three-stranded rope isn't easily snapped.

ECCLESIASTES 4:12

Okay, Todd, you may be thinking, *I am tracking with you—I think I get it. The Christian life is life in the kingdom, living as ambassadors of the kingdom. It is being the cooperative friends of Jesus, living in creative goodness for the sake of others through the power of the Holy Spirit. But what exactly can I do to implement this vision?* Well, I do have a way to get started.

A SIMPLE PRACTICE
Three Is Enough (TIE) groups are a simple way to practice following God in the way of Jesus. They are my way of implementing the ideas in this book. We have discussed a new way of thinking about what it means to be a Christian and a new way to live based on that understanding. Three Is Enough groups give us a practical way to do it.

"Three Is Enough" has a double meaning: (1) three friends or colleagues (2) doing three simple and humble activities. Functioning in places of daily life—the workplace, school, retirement home or local coffee shop—Three Is Enough groups go on the inward journey of spiritual transformation and the outward journey of serving others.

A friend of mine recently started a Three Is Enough group with two colleagues. Her story illustrates the power of a TIE group to give some minimal structure to live in a cooperative friendship with Jesus, in creative goodness for others. The following is an e-mail recounting the start-up of her TIE group:

> Todd,
>
> We had our first meeting this week and it went great. We are reading a book on spiritual warfare together as we decided that this type of group may come under attack ☺. Two quick examples of how we are being quickened to serving others.
>
> 1. As you may have seen on the news we recently had a fire in the foothills nearby. A lady in our group felt prompted to call the families in the immediate area and check on them and offer any help we could with their kids. All three families were very surprised we took the time to call, and were very grateful. One family actually said we were the ONLY people who called, and they were evacuating their house. What a small way to show love and caring ☺.
>
> 2. I then went to see one of my students. I was having the best time listening to the teacher guide the students through a lesson. When there was a small break before she started her next lesson, I felt like I was supposed to let her know how much I enjoyed watching her with the students. She isn't a teacher I am close with, as I spend most of my time with the case manager and the teaching assistant, so I don't really have any type of relationship with her. I just walked up and said to her, "I don't know if people tell you this enough but you are

a phenomenal teacher. I work with dozens of teachers a year and I love to watch you teach. These kids are very lucky." She teared up, gave me a hug and said, "You don't know how bad I needed to hear that right now. I have a lot going on and I think God sent you to me today to tell me that." I just said, "Well he does work in mysterious ways," and she went back to teach. Is this a taste of what is to come? Good grief. What a nice validation from God. Talk to you soon.

Can you see how the themes we have been considering come through in this story? Cooperative friends of Jesus (they started the TIE group to do this better), creatively doing good (calling families, speaking kind words), for the sake of others (fire victims and a struggling teacher), through the leading of the Holy Spirit (they were "quickened" to help, and led to speak certain words). I love the part about "validation from God." It's the coolest thing on earth to know that we are working with God for the sake of others—that we are living as God intended.

THREE IS ENOUGH ACTIVITIES

To put flesh on the idea of being the cooperative friends of Jesus for the sake of others, participants in Three Is Enough groups do three things:

1. *Pray* for alertness to the Spirit's leadership and guidance. Pray that we might pay attention to the people and events of our life. Pray that the Spirit will enable us to be ambassadors of the kingdom in the routines of our life. Pray for the ability to do good for others. And pray for the members of our group as we go on this journey.

2. *Grow* by reading material that facilitates the journey inward and the journey outward. Grow by meditating on the things the Spirit highlights in our reading. And grow by discussing our reading with our TIE group once a week.

3. *Serve* others by being alert, by noticing others. Serve others through creative, resourceful and inventive help. Serve others by being humble, gentle, generous and genuinely altruistic—we do not draw attention to ourselves or our TIE group. God desires that we become his cooperative friends—serving others—the least, the last, the broken and the oppressed—in the everyday affairs and rhythms of our life. If following Jesus means anything, it means serving others (Mark 10:41-45).

Three Is Enough groups are not an end in themselves. Once we've started on the inner journey and are sharing with our TIE partners what we are reading and learning, we start looking for small but meaningful ways to serve our community. While it takes some minimal facilitation along the way, it takes no special leadership for it to work and multiply. And the group can serve in any context. For example, several nurses could band together to do this on a hospital floor. They could pray when appropriate. They could serve grieving families. In short, their floor is no longer merely their place of work, it becomes the soil of their discipleship and missional engagement with the world.

Families living in the same apartment complex could do the same. They could babysit for exhausted two-income parents. They could help the elderly do some spring cleaning or pot some flowers. Three policemen could do the same on their shift. They could give practical aid to fellow officers whose families are feeling the strain of police work. They could care for young moms who have just given birth while their police-officer husbands are working. A few corporate parking-lot attendants could band together to pray for each employee as they drive in and out of the lot each work day.

A Three Is Enough group is like rails to run on. It provides the structure for being alert to the Spirit and paying attention to the people and events of our life. It guides our growth as we serve others.

WHY THREE IS ENOUGH GROUPS?

Most people are interested in the spiritual component of their life. Spiritual transformation into Christlikeness is the right thing to do, and the reputation of Christianity and thus effective evangelism hangs upon it. Current research shows that un-Christian, un-Christ-formed faith and practice is the single biggest obstacle to attracting new followers of Jesus.

People formerly listened their way into the faith; now they tend to talk and observe their way into the faith. Thus Jesus' followers' two primary roles in evangelism are listening and embodying authentic Christianity. By repracticing Christianity—that is, trading behaviors seen as patently hypocritical for a lifestyle in alignment with the kingdom—we can break the negative, "un-Christian" image of our faith.

In *The Fall of the Evangelical Nation* Christine Wicker argues that evangelical Christianity in America is dying. The book says that every indicator that can be measured shows great losses: in conversions, baptisms, attendance, giving, membership and participation.

Wicker says every day America is becoming a less Christian nation. The evangelical version of Christianity has dropped from 42 percent of the population in 1900 to 15 percent today. Twelve hundred evangelicals leave the faith each day; overall one thousand Christians leave the faith each day. Many of these people say they are leaving out of deep, Bible-inspired values. Twenty million believers are now getting their primary spiritual experience and nourishment through small groups. This is just the beginning of an ever-widening trend.

Wicker notes that, in numbers and percentages, nonbelievers are the fastest growing "faith" group in America. They outnumber evangelicals, more than two to one. When asked to evaluate groups in terms of respect, non-Christians rated evangelicals tenth. Only prostitutes ranked lower. We obviously need to do something, and fast.

I do not recount these grim statistics to bash the church or to set aside the importance of weekend gatherings of the church. Routine meetings are part of our human wiring. For instance, fill in these sentences in your mind: "I play golf every (Saturday). I play bridge every (Wednesday)." Lunar rhythms were built into creaturely life long before we had churches. Why fight these innate rhythms? Why not make them work on behalf of spiritual formation?

Wicker asserts that the core group of people volunteering at churches wants a deeper commitment to faith, one that extends beyond church walls. They want to live their faith in everything they do—work and play.

Three Is Enough groups are a great way to express our faith in everything we do. Rooting the practices of Christianity in daily life and community is at the heart of TIE groups. With TIE I am trying to give us an imagination for the church scattered with the confidence that such a synergistic practice (gathered then scattered) will help us better follow Jesus for the sake of others.

The time is ripe for a fresh approach to spiritual formation—one that is based in real life. If we can connect spiritual formation to serving others, we will not only correct Christianity's poor image but, even more significant, facilitate authentic, relationally sound evangelism. Three Is Enough removes spiritual formation and evangelism from church programming and puts it back into daily life.

VALUES OF THREE IS ENOUGH GROUPS

The following are some values to guide us as we begin a Three Is Enough group.

- Choosing to be his apprentices, we value our relationship with Jesus, our Lord and Master, who teaches us how to be faithful children of God for the sake of others.

- We value the Holy Spirit as our guide and source of character and power. We will interact with him in conversational ways without hype or pretense.

- We will strive to carry out the practices associated with our group, but we don't want to confuse this effort with earning God's love. Grace is for the whole journey of discipleship, not just conversion.

- We will focus on and immerse ourselves in the righteousness, peace and joy of the kingdom, replacing neurotic religious guilt, shame or fear with this reality.

- This life matters, not just the life to come. Therefore the events and people of our life are of utmost value.

- Neither spiritual formation nor a missional engagement with our world can be added to an already too-busy or out-of-control life. We follow Jesus for the sake of others within the existing contexts, rhythms and routines of our present life, not some hoped-for life that will never come.

- We believe every Christ-follower should be oriented toward serving others.

- When God asks us to be his cooperative friends, he will provide the motivation and means to do so.

- We will look for those who may be ready to enter life in the kingdom, making Jesus and his kingdom teachings known.

- Our Three Is Enough group is not an end in itself. The group's *telos* is following Jesus as ambassadors of the kingdom's goodness for the sake of others.

- We will not be spiritual police, office nags or creepy religious types.

- We will practice our faith with gentleness, humility and in hidden service to others.

- The journey outward doesn't begin after getting our act together. Therefore, we won't wait till we're fully "fixed" before starting our lives of creative goodness. Some things about us can't be learned apart from first taking the risk of loving and serving others.

- Our group will not criticize the church. It is designed to help the church be the sent people of God in daily life.

STARTING A THREE IS ENOUGH GROUP

To start a Three Is Enough group, invite two colleagues who want to grow as Christians (or who are spiritual seekers) to join you on a spiritual journey. Most people are trying to make sense of life, and they believe everyday spirituality is a way to get there.

Meet once a week for thirty to sixty minutes (for breakfast, lunch or evening coffee). This time allows you to swap wonderful or scary stories, to discuss what you are reading, to share what you are learning about yourself or others, and to pray for each other.

A comprehensive list of frequently asked questions regarding TIE groups can be found in appendix 4. (Check www.3isenough.com for additional information supplied by TIE groups from around the world.)

GUIDELINES FOR PARTICIPATION IN A THREE IS ENOUGH GROUP

A Three Is Enough group is meant to be relaxed, even fun. Belonging to one is an adventure, a discovery of the profound inner life which exists in all of us; it's about learning to notice others; and most importantly it's about discovering a life derived from and lived in the kingdom of God.

Make sure you have a vision larger than participation in a TIE group. A TIE group is simply the means for carrying out our vision and intention to be humanity as God intended, to be a follower of Jesus for the sake of others.

The crucial points of participation include:

- *Trying new ways to pray.* A quiet time that doesn't carry forward in the attitudes and actions of our life can be reinvigorated by experimenting with situational and conversational forms of prayer rooted in the people and events of your life. Though I pray most mornings (simply orienting myself to God as his cooperative friend and dedicating my day to him) and almost every evening, I do very simple things throughout the day that have revolutionized my life.

Try developing some prayers that you use throughout the day. When you pick up the phone, pray, "May the words of my mouth and meditations of my heart be acceptable to you in this conversation." Or when you have an appointment with someone, pray, "May I be really present to this person." Before most any activity the prayer "May your kingdom come and may your will be done" is appropriate.

I know this sounds like anyone can do it—and they can! That and the fact that it actually connects us to God and his purposes is what makes it real and vibrant.

- *Read and interact.* This should only take a few minutes a day and then thirty to sixty minutes per week with your TIE group. Remember, the point is neither to be in a group nor to see how much you can read or how long you meet with your group. The point is spiritual transformation into Christlikeness for the sake of others.

    The group could mutually agree to read something together, or each member could read material targeted to his or her needs or curiosity. Each person then reports back to the group how the reading is helping him or her follow Jesus for the sake of others.

    Let's be real. We already know more about ourselves, others and God than we can apply. That is part of the frustration about being a Christian. (It's also what the watching world judges us by.) So we shouldn't feel pressure to read large amounts. Smaller, consistently targeted material is sufficient. If patience is our problem, then we should focus on authors and writings that help us be patient. And we shouldn't feel the need to quickly move on to the next thing— even if someone in the group seems to be going faster.

Keep in mind the learning curve of the first disciples ("Is Jesus mad because we forgot bread again?" or "Why couldn't we cast this demon out?"). They learned at different rates, and each of them stumbled and fell. Nevertheless, as the cooperative friends of Jesus and through the presence and power of the Spirit, they changed the course of history!

- *Serve others in creative and genuinely helpful ways.* A Three Is Enough group may decide to dig wells for clean water in Africa—that is great! But the more immediate goal is to learn to do similar things in the context of our everyday lives where we live, work and play.

  This is done by training, not merely by trying. No couch potato would try to run a marathon without training—it simple can't be done. But starting little by little—by first regularly walking, then progressing to jogging and finally running, it's conceivable a couch potato could become a marathoner. Through God's grace and the power of the Spirit, spiritual transformation works in a similar manner.

The TIE group provides ways to practice serving others in the daily routines of life. We don't need to fly overseas or even to another part of our country. We start by being present to the people and events of our regular life. When we notice them, by taking them into our heart and mind, then wide vistas of opportunity will open up to us.

The drama and excitement that will soon follow is hard to imagine. I know many people who live this way, and I've lived it myself. In addition to our daily duties, we continually listen to the hearts of others and the leading of the Holy Spirit. This may seem impossible. But trust me, it's not difficult to concentrate on your job, paying attention to the people and events within that work, *and* to the leading of the Holy Spirit.

With practice it becomes as natural as tossing a ball or cleaning dishes while talking to a friend. I'm not a big fan of multitasking.

While allegedly making us more productive, I think it has worsened the human condition in some ways, making some of us a little neurotic. That's not my goal. I have something like the following in mind: picture a nurse waiting to get a reading from a patient's monitor. As she waits, she focuses on the patient and God. That's all. We can't make anything happen. All we can do is pay attention through the Golden Triangle of Presence (see p. 105). And once we do this, we'll be amazed at what people and the Holy Spirit reveal to us. I envision this happening as Jesus said, "Walk with me and work with me— watch how I do it. Learn the unforced rhythms of grace. I won't lay anything heavy or ill-fitting on you. Keep company with me and you'll learn to live freely and lightly" (Matthew 11:29-30).

Three Is Enough groups, focused on discipleship (the inner and outer journeys), can happen as Jesus said. Remember, the key is not adding a bunch of new stuff to our life, further cluttering it with busyness. Rather, we learn to follow Jesus in our already-established life.

For many of us we will practice our discipleship at our workplace. So let me give a couple of practical tips rooted in my years of experience with this. First, what I am advocating should never lead to poor work but a better you, and thus better work. Second, it should be done as quietly as possible. I'm not suggesting lying about what you are doing, only that not drawing attention to ourself has a long tradition in Christian spirituality.

In the Sermon on the Mount, Jesus says two apparently contradictory things. In the first text Jesus encourages his followers to let their lights shine before others so that these others, seeing our good works, will glorify God.

> You're here to be light, bringing out the God-colors in the world. God is not a secret to be kept. We're going public with this, as public as a city on a hill. If I make you light-bearers, you don't think I'm going to hide you under a bucket, do you? I'm putting

you on a light stand. Now that I've put you there on a hilltop, on a light stand—shine! Keep open house; be generous with your lives. By opening up to others, you'll prompt people to open up with God. (Matthew 5:14-16)

One chapter later he seems to contradict himself.

Be especially careful when you are trying to be good so that you don't make a performance out of it. . . . When you help someone out, don't think about how it looks. Just do it—quietly and unobtrusively. That is the way your God, who conceived you in love, working behind the scenes, helps you out. (Matthew 6:1, 3-4)

I've always wanted to shout "Which is it?" at those two texts! Here is the way I have worked it out. In the second instance Jesus is correcting the religious leaders of his day who were doing religious deeds so that others would think highly of them. That of course solidified their power over the people, which was their goal. This is why Jesus rebukes them for putting heavy loads on the people while not lifting a finger to help them with their already "heavy load of life."

In the first instance, I hear Jesus saying something like, "Serving others is what you were created for. This is an old story. It goes back to the calling of Abraham and the forming of Israel to be my others-oriented people, my agents of healing and reconciliation in the world. When you act in ways that are congruent with that story, constantly living in creative goodness as my cooperative friends, you bring glory to God; you affirm and make manifest the goodness and rightness of his plan." I'm finding that though Three Is Enough groups focus on God and others, group members benefit as much as anyone. The following e-mail from a friend who works for a large corporation shines a light on this TIE overflow.

Hey there, Todd!
Every week I look forward to meeting with Carol. The conver-

sations are so honest and transparent that this one, small, sixty-minute lunch break during the week feels like drinking deeply from a fresh-water spring. It's simply rejuvenating to both of us.

I knew when I asked Carol to be the first to join the TIE group that she was a believer, but I wasn't sure where in her faith walk she was. Nor did she know where I stood. Therefore, we decided to make it a group of two so that we could learn more about one another and better discern who else to ask. Currently, we are enjoying one another's company so much that we decided not to ask a third person to join us, at least for now.

Prior to your asking us if we'd like to participate, I recently had a close friendship at work become difficult and somewhat impact my focus in the office because I had been so hurt by it. In January, I made a conscious decision not to make close friends with anyone in the workplace, but to come in, do my job to the best of my ability, and leave so as not to become entangled emotionally with my coworkers. The prior experience had just been too painful.

Although I was bubbling over with excitement to start a TIE group, I was also a bit apprehensive, for it meant going back on my vow with myself in regards to close friendships in the office. The one part of the equation that had been missing before was a common denominator rooted in a love of and for Christ. I am so glad in just these four weeks that I did break that vow, because I am richly benefiting from this budding new friendship in Christ.

Our first week we spent our time sharing about our faith journey. We shared how the Holy Spirit has guided us and where our challenges ahead lay. The second week we decided to read *Prince Caspian* so that we could later discuss the film. Last week we read *Hung by the Tongue* and discussed the power that speech holds. That book was incredibly convicting and we shared how challenging it is in the workplace to speak affirmatively and to not use our tongue as a weapon by speaking ill of others whom we feel challenge us.

Our conversations are positive, uplifting, and supporting, as we encourage one another in our walk and how to be better followers of Christ to those around us at work, home, and elsewhere.

An example of the listening/paying attention came when Carol had noticed that one of our security hosts (Betty) didn't seem as upbeat as she normally is. Carol took a few minutes out of her day to hear about how Betty had become seriously ill and had to be rushed to the hospital for an emergency procedure. Carol listened attentively and said she would keep Betty in her thoughts. At lunch, Carol shared the news with me, and I was able to find Betty and follow up on her progress, and also say that I would be keeping her in my thoughts. It felt a kind gesture to do for the security hosts who often may feel overlooked at Disney since they aren't always considered part of the staff.

Carol and I are so sad to be missing two weeks of our lunches while I am away in Europe, but we'll both be reading our next book on Spiritual Warfare.

It's been such a blessing to reach out and have a transparent and genuine relationship in our little department of 20 people. After the difficulty with the other friendship at work, I felt it impossible to have any intimate and transparent friendships in the office. God is the only variable that can make that happen, I think.

CURLY'S FINGER

This past weekend my wife and I went "old school" in search of a comedy to watch. We were feeling too lazy to go to a theater; in fact we were even too lethargic to go out to rent a movie. (How pathetic!) Rummaging around our collection of DVDs we noticed *City Slickers*.

We were in the mood to laugh and had not watched this movie in years, so we loaded it into the player. If you've seen it, you undoubtedly remember big, bad Curly telling Mitch, the character played by Billy Crystal, that the secret to life "is just one thing."

I don't have a big secret to share with you, but I do have one last word of advice: It is important that we bind TIE groups to grace and wisdom. There is a lot we could do in these groups to bring on legitimate criticism. But no one will object to unobtrusive, others-oriented service that loves others with no expectation of recognition or repayment. This will bring God's dream to pass. We will indeed be his light on a hill—his cooperative friends. We will have moved from mere beliefs to following Jesus for the sake of others.

FOR REFLECTION AND DISCUSSION

1. What do you think of the structure of Three Is Enough groups?

2. Do you think being a member of a TIE group would be helpful to you? Why or why not? What is most worrisome to you about the group? (Please go to www.3isenough.com if you've got some constructive criticism.)

3. What would it take for you to start a TIE group? (If you need more help, please go to the website mentioned in question 1.)

4. Which of the three practices (pray, read, serve) do you think you would do best with? Which would be hardest? Why? What spiritual discipline would empower you to carry out the difficult practice?

APPENDIX 1

TRIADS: The Theoretical Basis
for Three Is Enough Groups

I first heard the term *triad* from my friend Bob Logan. As I began to work on this book the idea came back to me. I like the concept of triads, which I will soon explain in detail, not just because their value is proven but also because they are fluid; thus they fit our transitory times. Things change; people come and go. Triads can be and often are modified as members come and go. And this is not all bad—it allows the practice of Three Is Enough groups to spread to a new city or workplace.

Greg Ogden, a highly respected pastoral voice in the area of discipleship, has also written on the use of triads. InterVarsity Press kindly sent me two of Greg's books to review. A summary of his thoughts follow too.

As an aside, I also hear that the Cursillo movement uses a simple three-step method (a triad) to help their members. The three steps are piety, study and action—very close to the TIE steps. These examples confirm that I have not come up with some novel, untested idea. Without previously knowing it, my idea stands in a long line of effective tools.

A BRIEF HISTORY OF TRIADS FROM BOB LOGAN'S *COACHING 101*

As I was writing chapter ten, I contacted Bob Logan and asked him to help me better articulate the triad concept. What follows are some seminal thoughts from Bob's writings and a few notes I took from our call.

A few years ago I [Bob] was consulting with a denomination that wanted to design a comprehensive coaching process. They'd already done a lot of coaching with their church planters, but until now had not applied it to the pastors of existing churches. As I dialogued with the pastors, I sensed their reluctance to form one-on-one coaching relationships with each other. They were concerned about pride and competition for the mentor/coach role. They viewed coaching as supervisory, and didn't believe it could be experienced as a peer relationship.

That's when I introduced triads. Triads are excellent for peer coaching relationships, and can be one of the least intimidating options for those just getting started as coaches. By meeting together with two other beginning coaches, you can take risks and try out new ideas in a safe, non-threatening environment. Triads are the perfect place to practice, develop, and hone your coaching skills, gaining the confidence necessary to take those skills into other areas of life.

Here's how they work [this is how Bob used them to coach pastoral leaders]: three leaders meet for an hour and a half in person once a month. These three leaders have already been trained in basic coaching skills. Each leader gets half an hour to talk about whatever he or she wants. Meanwhile, the other two leaders provide good listening, questions, and feedback, then lay hands on and pray. No focus shifting is allowed; it is not free-form discussion, but a disciplined process within a structured timeframe.

One group of pastors who formed a coaching triad found immediate and powerful results. Needs started being met as they experienced the power of a caring and supportive community. The pastors were amazed at what a rare gift it was to receive half an hour of focused attention and the opportunity to process without interruptions or someone saying, "Here's what happened to me . . ." This brief exercise of only an hour and a half a month gave them each a taste of what coaching could be, along with a sense of excitement that they could pass this gift along to others.

Furthermore, Bob explained to me:

> Six out of the seven triads that were formed that day met every month and the reviews were phenomenal. They found that peer coaching in triads takes off the pressure. They didn't have to have the answer; they just had to listen, summarize, and ask good questions.

Later, Bob discovered that triads can also be used for accountability groups, for spiritual-formation groups and life-transformation groups. As an example, Bob connected me to Tom Clegg. Tom is a highly regarded missionary, pastor and church consultant, president of Coach-Net and a senior consultant for Outreach, Inc. In his "How to Plant a Church" seminar, he shares from his experience of triads in an accountability group:

> My accountability group is a triad, and that has been our format for the last fourteen years. Six people are involved, so we use two groups of three. We meet every other week at a tea house. We've found that this system works very effectively. You can fake out one person, but you can't fake out two. You can't dodge the subject, or get away from the issue. That's the genius of the triads in my opinion.

Tom's church planters are now using this system for accountability as well:

Our church planters have now been using triads for two years, and the planters that do it don't go back. It's simple, idiot-proof, and powerful. By using triads, it doesn't come down to one planter's personal opinion or style of ministry or culture. Three can get at the deeper heart of the matter more readily than two.

His local church has begun using triads for spiritual formation:

Triads worked so well with our planters that I introduced it in our local church as well. It started with just a few guys involved in the men's ministry. In triads, they found the accessible, direct ministry they had always longed for. Especially since our church had no small groups at the time, triads filled a huge need. Beginning in the men's ministry, a small high-trust subculture emerged, and then went on to impact the larger body. The system has since multiplied and it's how we do spiritual formation. It does require some maintenance, oversight, and encouragement—someone to take responsibility to facilitate them—but generally, the triads function in a leaderless fashion.

Bob relates another story that comes from Neil Cole, pastor of Awakening Chapel. He started a cell church to reach people who didn't know Christ. Their follow-up system for new converts is very simple: life-transformation groups. No training is needed. Two to four people come together regularly for Scripture reading and accountability. Started just five years ago, life-transformation groups are now functioning on all seven continents.

The phrase Neil uses to describe his philosophy of ministry is, "First things first. One thing at a time. Always one more thing." He helps people grow step by step into leadership, raising up leaders from among the converts through a continual discipleship and mentoring process.

GREG OGDEN ON TRIADS

Greg Ogden has written two books in which he recommends the use of triads: *Discipleship Essentials: A Guide to Building Your Life in Christ* and *Transforming Discipleship: Making Disciples a Few at a Time.*

The following are some keys points in his books. (My comments are in parentheses.)

1. Triads are ever-expanding, multigenerational and reproducible.

2. Triads allow a group to convene around a simple covenant (like the one I suggest in chap. 10).

3. Greg has deeply studied a variety of contexts for discipleship: (1) one-on-one (which, he says, often end up feeling like hierarchical parent-child or teacher-student relationships)‡ and (2) small groups up to ten members. In Greg's judgment triads are superior because

   - Dependency on a single leader is broken in a triad. Leadership and responsibility are felt by the whole group. (I believe this is crucial for the spread of any movement and is a vital reason I chose to develop Three Is Enough groups.)

   - Triads are relational and avoid the parent-child and teacher-student hierarchy. (A teacher often learns more in the classroom than the students. Triads allow for teaching and insight to be shared by all. This is a powerful force for leadership development.)

   - Triads allow for more dialogue and perspective than one-on-one pairings.

   - Three is a good-feeling number. Triads provide the best sense of groupness.

   - Triads provide room for the Spirit to be manifestly present.

   - There is more potential to multiply in a triad than in one-on-one or small groups.

---

‡I, Todd, know many people in the generation before me for whom one-on-one worked well, so maybe Greg's view represents a generational shift?

4. Triads allow for greater flexibility in choosing settings, meeting times, duration of the group, service opportunities and so on.

5. Triads focus accountability around life change. (I would add *for the sake of others*. Other programs tend to focus on content, not life change or practices.)

6. Triads are positive, grace-giving reciprocal environments for encouragement, equipping, practicing various spiritual disciplines and mutual challenge.

Conclusion. Greg was caught off-guard by his research, which revealed the life-changing dynamics of triads versus one-to-one relationships. As he examined this dynamic further, he discovered that in triads there is a shift

- from unnatural pressure to natural participation,
- from dialogue to dynamic interchange,
- from limited input to wisdom in numbers, and
- from addition to multiplication.

APPENDIX 2

The Person and Work of the Holy Spirit

The biblical revelation of God, as understood and taught by the historic church, is that God is triune: one God eternally coexisting in three persons. The Holy Spirit is often called the third person of the Trinity, which doesn't mean the Spirit is third in importance. The Scriptures make clear the deity of the Holy Spirit. He is called God (Acts 5:3-4); he is joined with the Father and Son (Matthew 28:19; 2 Corinthians 13:14; 1 John 5:7); he is eternal (Hebrews 9:14), omnipotent (Luke 1:35), omniscient (1 Corinthians 2:10-11), omnipresent (Psalm 139:7-13) and sovereign (1 Corinthians 12:6, 11). The Holy Spirit makes present and real the work of God in the world. This is especially true after the resurrection of Jesus. The Spirit is the promised continuing presence of Jesus in the church—the people of God.

It is a sad reality that in our days the Holy Spirit has too often become a controversial doctrine rather than a highly sought and prized presence, God's ongoing provision of himself. He never leaves us orphaned or spiritually impotent (John 14:16-26). The Father and Son have sometimes dominated the thinking and imagination of contemporary Christians—almost to the point of ignoring the person and work of the Holy Spirit.

This is true for at least two reasons: (1) some people are afraid of falling into excess regarding the Spirit, and (2) the modern, scientific, material worldview has little capacity for interacting with incorporeal, personal power. The empirical view has trouble comprehending this divine person who has no body and yet is ultimate power. Thus, even though many Christians don't deny the Spirit's existence, they often steer clear of any meaningful interaction with him.

In contrast, the story of Scripture reveals that the Holy Spirit interacts personally with humanity. From creation (Genesis 1:1-2; Psalm 104:30) to the new heavens and the new earth (Revelation 22:17), the Spirit equips various agents of God (Numbers 11:16-17; Judges 14:1-6; Micah 3:8), is active in the birth of Jesus (Luke 1:35), is a dynamic actor in redemption (John 3:3-5; Romans 15:16; 2 Thessalonians 2:13), enables writing of Scripture (2 Timothy 3:14-17; 2 Peter 1:19-21), teaches and leads into truth (John 16:8, 13; 1 John 2:20), and gives discernment (1 Corinthians 2:10-16; 1 John 4:1-6). The Spirit fills, empowers and animates Christian life (John 14:15-31; Acts 2:1-41; Romans 8:1-27; 14:17; 1 Corinthians 2:6-16; Galatians 5:16-26). The Spirit produces the character of Christ (Galatians 5:22-23) and gifts the church for service to others—both those in and outside of the church (Romans 12:3-8; Ephesians 4:7-13; 1 Corinthians 12:3-11). The Spirit leads and guides the work of the church (Acts 8:29; 13:2, 4; 20:17-28).

Meaningful interaction with the Holy Spirit is found in the Scriptures. They depict the Spirit with personal attributes: speaking (Acts 28:25), teaching (John 14:26), comforting (Acts 9:31), recognizing and helping our weaknesses (Romans 8:26), being grieved (Ephesians 4:30), being resisted (Acts 7:51), and lied to (Acts 5:3). Church history is filled with testimonies of the difference-making experience of being filled with the Spirit. These testimonies include those thought of as model Christians: John Wesley, George Whitefield, George Fox, Charles Spurgeon, Martin Luther, Dwight L. Moody, Billy Graham, Mother Teresa and General William Booth of the Salvation Army.

WORKING WITH THE HOLY SPIRIT

Various theological traditions have understood the relationship between the individual Christian and the Holy Spirit in different ways. Some see reception of the Spirit occurring simultaneously with conversion. Others see initiation into an interactive life with the Holy Spirit as a second event that occurs after conversion. Among the latter group are Pentecostals, who believe that the initial sign of Spirit reception is the gift of speaking in tongues.

There are five instances in the book of Acts where individuals or groups are filled with the Spirit. In two of the cases they spoke in tongues (Acts 2:4; 10:46). In one case they spoke in tongues and prophesied (Acts 19:6). In one case we are not told what happened, but obviously something visible or audible happened (Acts 8:14-19). In Paul's case he received healing and his commissioning (Acts 9:17). Thus we can say that when people are filled with the Spirit, various manifestations of the Spirit occur. The crucial bit, no matter what the first sign is, is the knowledge that God is truly with us, empowering us to live a Spirit-filled life for the sake of serving others as the cooperative friends of God.

The question is often asked, "How can I be filled with the Holy Spirit?" If we take the position that a convert receives the Spirit at conversion, the reception of the Spirit is better seen as actualizing what is already possessed. If Spirit reception is seen as sequential, it is a fresh experience. In either case, the way to receive the Spirit is to simply ask in faith; sincerely desiring to be guided and empowered by God the Holy Spirit. You can be sure that God will give what you ask (Luke 11:9-13).

God gives the Spirit because Spirit power is essential to life as a Christian—for life as an ambassador of the kingdom (2 Corinthians 5:17-21). While human effort is part of life as ambassadors of the kingdom, kingdom work is never merely human. When we ignore the person and work of the Spirit, arrogance, burnout and frustration directed at others is sure to follow. The Spirit was given to the church to allow it to be the people of God.

The Holy Spirit is not *in* the life of the church, nor does he merely *create* the life of the church. He *is* the life of the church. He is the animating, energizing, empowering, gift-giving, fruit-bearing power that makes the church real and alive. There is no church without the Holy Spirit. The Spirit creates, leads and guides the work of the church.

Spiritual experiences might be pleasurable, but such pleasure is not the sole or even main point. Just as the Spirit descended on Jesus in fullness at his baptism (Matthew 3:16-17) to fulfill his role as Messiah, the Spirit enables the church to be the cooperative people of God in the world, empowering it to continue the work of Jesus, to spread his victory over the forces of evil in the world—announcing, embodying and demonstrating the rule and reign of God on behalf of all fallen creation, which has gone astray from the purposes of God.

Also note that because he is a person, the Spirit can be grieved or quenched (Ephesians 4:30; 1 Thessalonians 5:19). While some Christians do all they can to avoid excesses related to the person and work of the Spirit, the Spirit is equally grieved by being ignored, set aside or resisted. Being open is not enough. Having enough faith and desire to ask is needed (Luke 11:9-13).

How do we best cooperate with the third person of the Trinity? We must avoid two traps: (1) a scientific, empirical mindset that excludes such possibilities, and (2) religious excesses, especially selfish ones that harm people and bring disrepute to the church and God.

The process of seeking and growing in the Spirit is made safe and sane with a heart to obey and the childlike determination to learn as we go. Our interactive relationship with the Spirit in our everyday life, as promised by John the Baptist and Jesus (Matthew 3:11; Luke 24:49; Acts 1:4-5), is maintained by practicing the presence. We learn to pay attention, to be alert to the Spirit, trusting that he will teach us to interact with him in ways that are good for others and honoring of God.

For Further Reading

Grudem, Wayne. *Systematic Theology*. Grand Rapids: Zondervan, 1994.

Fee, Gordon D. *Paul, the Spirit and the People of God*. Peabody, Mass.: Hendrickson, 1996.

—————. *God's Empowering Presence: The Holy Spirit in the Letters of Paul*. Peabody, Mass.: Hendrickson, 1994.

APPENDIX 3

THE MESSAGE: A New Testament Tour of Life

Throughout this book I have cast a vision for a Christianity that is primarily about our actual present life: a new kind of life that starts at the point of faith and followership of Jesus. While this new life also changes our eventual death and eternity, in order to be a follower of Jesus for the sake of others, we need a vision for how the gospel of the kingdom renovates our life now.

Below is a selection of biblical passages from *The Message* translation of Scripture. They highlight "life." I commend them to you for study, consideration, meditation and discussion in Three Is Enough groups.

These passages have shaped my imagination for a new kind of life. I hope they do the same for you.

■ ■ ■

There at the Jordan River those who came to confess their sins were baptized into a changed life. . . .

It's your life that must change. . . . What counts is your life. . . .

I'm baptizing you here in the river, turning your old life in for a kingdom life. . . . [Jesus] will ignite kingdom life within you . . . the Holy Spirit within you, changing you from the inside out. [He'll] . . . make a clean sweep of your lives. He'll place everything true in its proper place before God. (Matthew 3:6, 8, 10-12)

*[Jesus] picked up where John left off: "Change your life. God's
kingdom is here." . . .*

*God's kingdom was his theme—that beginning right now they were
under God's government, a good government! (Matthew 4:17, 23)*

*You're kingdom subjects. Now live like it. Live out your God-created
identity. Live generously and graciously toward others, the way God lives
toward you. (Matthew 5:48)*

*These words I speak to you are not incidental additions to your
life, homeowner improvements to your standard of living. They are
foundational words, words to build a life on. (Matthew 7:24)*

*Another follower said, "Master, excuse me for a couple of days, please. I
have my father's funeral to take care of."*

*Jesus refused. "First things first. Your business is life, not death. Follow
me. Pursue life." (Matthew 8:21-22)*

*Are you tired? Worn out? Burned out on religion? Come to me. Get away
with me and you'll recover your life. I'll show you how to take a real rest.
Walk with me and work with me—watch how I do it. Learn the unforced
rhythms of grace. I won't lay anything heavy or ill-fitting on you. Keep
company with me and you'll learn to live freely and lightly.
(Matthew 11:28-30)*

*When Jonah preached to them [the Ninevites] they changed their lives.
(Matthew 12:41)*

*Self-sacrifice is the way, my way to finding yourself, your true self.
(Matthew 16:25)*

God authorized and commanded me to commission you: Go out and train everyone you meet, far and near, in this way of life, marking them by baptism in the threefold name: Father, Son, and Holy Spirit. Then instruct them in the practice of all I have commanded you. I'll be with you as you do this, day after day after day, right up to the end of the age. (Matthew 28:18-20)

John the Baptizer appeared in the wild, preaching a baptism of life-change that leads to forgiveness of sins. People thronged to him from Judea and Jerusalem and, as they confessed their sins, were baptized by him in the Jordan River into a changed life. . . .

As he preached he said, "The real action comes next: The star in this drama, to whom I'm a mere stagehand, will change your life. I'm baptizing you here in the river, turning your old life in for a kingdom life. His baptism—a holy baptism by the Holy Spirit—will change you from the inside out." . . .

Jesus went to Galilee preaching the Message of God: "Time's up! God's kingdom is here. Change your life and believe the Message." (Mark 1:4-5, 7-8, 14-15)

[The disciples] preached with joyful urgency that life can be radically different. (Mark 6:12)

[John preached] a baptism of life-change leading to forgiveness of sins. . . .

When crowds of people came out for baptism because it was the popular thing to do, John exploded: "Brood of snakes! What do you think you're doing slithering down here to the river? Do you think a little water on your snakeskins is going to deflect God's judgment? It's your life that must change, not your skin. And don't think you can pull rank by claiming Abraham as 'father.' Being a child of Abraham is neither here nor there—

children of Abraham are a dime a dozen. God can make children from stones if he wants. What counts is your life. Is it green and blossoming? Because if it's deadwood, it goes on the fire." (Luke 3:3, 7-9)

[Jesus said to the leper he had just healed,] "Your cleansed and obedient life, not your words, will bear witness to what I have done." . . .

Jesus heard about it [the controversy surrounding him] and spoke up, "Who needs a doctor: the healthy or the sick? I'm here inviting outsiders, not insiders—an invitation to a changed life, changed inside and out. (Luke 5:14, 31-32)

You don't get wormy apples off a healthy tree, nor good apples off a diseased tree. The health of the apple tells the health of the tree. You must begin with your own life-giving lives. It's who you are, not what you say and do, that counts. Your true being brims over into true words and deeds.

Why are you so polite with me, always saying "Yes, sir," and "That's right, sir," but never doing a thing I tell you? These words I speak to you are not mere additions to your life, homeowner improvements to your standard of living. They are foundation words, words to build a life on.

If you work the words into your life, you are like a smart carpenter who dug deep and laid the foundation of his house on bedrock. When the river burst its banks and crashed against the house, nothing could shake it; it was built to last. But if you just use my words in Bible studies and don't work them into your life, you are like a dumb carpenter who built a house but skipped the foundation. When the swollen river came crashing in, it collapsed like a house of cards. It was a total loss. (Luke 6:43-49)

Jesus said, . . . "Unless a person submits to this original creation—the 'wind-hovering-over-the-water' creation, the invisible moving the visible, a baptism into a new life—it's not possible to enter God's kingdom. . . .

[I]t is necessary for the Son of Man to be lifted up—and everyone who looks up to him, trusting and expectant, will gain a real life, eternal life.

This is how much God loved the world: He gave his Son, his one and only Son. And this is why: so that no one need be destroyed; by believing in him, anyone can have a whole and lasting life. . . .

[W]hoever accepts and trusts the Son gets in on everything, life complete and forever! (John 3:5, 14-17, 35)

The Son gives life to anyone he chooses. . . .

It's urgent that you listen carefully to this: Anyone here who believes what I am saying right now and aligns himself with the Father, who has in fact put me in charge, has at this very moment the real, lasting life and is no longer condemned to be an outsider. This person has taken a giant step from the world of the dead to the world of the living. . . .

You have your heads in your Bibles constantly because you think you'll find eternal life there. But you miss the forest for the trees. These Scriptures are all about me! And here I am, standing right before you, and you aren't willing to receive from me the life you say you want.
(John 5:21, 24, 39-40)

I came so they can have real and eternal life, more and better life than they ever dreamed of. (John 10:10)

Cut to the quick, those who were there listening asked Peter and the other apostles, "Brothers! Brothers! So now what do we do?"

Peter said, "Change your life. Turn to God and be baptized, each of you, in the name of Jesus Christ, so your sins are forgiven. Receive the gift of the Holy Spirit." (Acts 2:37-38)

That means you must not give sin a vote in the way you conduct your lives. Don't give it the time of day. Don't even run little errands that are connected with that old way of life. Throw yourselves wholeheartedly and full-time—remember, you've been raised from the dead!—into God's way of doing things. Sin can't tell you how to live. After all, you're not living under that old tyranny any longer. You're living in the freedom of God. . . .

You can readily recall, can't you, how at one time the more you did just what you felt like doing—not caring about others, not caring about God—the worse your life became the less freedom you had? And how much different is it now as you live in God's freedom, your lives healed and expansive in holiness? . . .

[N]ow that you've found you don't have to listen to sin tell you what to do, and have discovered the delight of listening to God telling you, what a surprise! A whole, healed, put-together life right now, with more and more of life on the way! Work hard for sin your whole life and your pension is death. But God's gift is real life, eternal life, delivered by Jesus, our Master. (Romans 6:12-14, 19, 22-23)

Those who enter into Christ's being-here-for-us no longer have to live under a continuous, low-lying black cloud. A new power is in operation. The Spirit of life in Christ, like a strong wind, has magnificently cleared the air, freeing you from a fated lifetime of brutal tyranny at the hands of sin and death. . . .

In his Son, Jesus, he personally took on the human condition, entered the disordered mess of struggling humanity in order to set it right once and for all. (Romans 8:1-3)

Obsession with self in these matters is a dead end; attention to God leads us out into the open, into a spacious, free life. . . .

God himself has taken up residence in your life, . . . for you who welcome him, in whom he dwells—even though you still experience all the *limitations of sin—you yourself experience life on God's terms. (Romans 8:6, 9-10)*

This resurrection life you received from God is not a timid, grave-tending life. It's adventurously expectant, greeting God with a childlike "What's next, Papa?" . . .

God knew what he was doing from the very beginning. He decided from the outset to shape the lives of those who love him along the same lines as the life of his Son. The Son stands first in the line of humanity he restored. We see the original and intended shape of our lives there in him. After God made that decision of what his children should be like, he followed it up by calling people by name. After he called them by name, he set them on a solid basis with himself. And then, after getting them established, he stayed with them to the end, gloriously completing what he had begun. (Romans 8:15, 29-30)

So here's what I want you to do, God helping you: Take your everyday, ordinary life—your sleeping, eating, going-to-work, and walking-around life—and place it before God as an offering. Embracing what God does for you is the best thing you can do for him. Don't become so well-adjusted to your culture that you fit into it without even thinking. Instead, fix your attention on God. You'll be changed from the inside out. Readily recognize what he wants from you, and quickly respond to it. Unlike the culture around you, always dragging you down to its level of immaturity, God brings the best out of you, develops well-formed maturity in you. (Romans 12:1-2)

The Messiah has made things up between us. . . . [H]e created a new kind of human being, a fresh start for everybody. (Ephesians 2:14-15)

*But that's no life for you. . . . [E]verything—and I do mean everything—
connected with that old way of life has to go. It's rotten through and
through. Get rid of it! And then take on an entirely new way of life—a
God-fashioned life, a life renewed from the inside and working itself into
your conduct as God accurately reproduces his character in you.
(Ephesians 4:20, 22-24)*

*Be energetic in your life of salvation, reverent and sensitive before God.
(Philippians 2:12)*

*Your old life is dead. Your new life, which is your real life—even though
invisible to spectators—is with Christ in God. He is your life. When
Christ (your real life, remember) shows up again on this earth, you'll show
up, too—the real you, the glorious you. (Colossians 3:3-4)*

*So, chosen by God for this new life of love, dress in the wardrobe God
picked out for you: compassion, kindness, humility, quiet strength,
discipline. Be even-tempered, content with second place, quick to forgive an
offense. Forgive as quickly and completely as the Master forgave you. And
regardless of what else you put on, wear love. It's your basic, all-purpose
garment. Never be without it. (Colossians 3:12-14)*

*Live well, live wisely, live humbly. It's the way you live, not the way you
talk, that counts. (James 3:13)*

*Because Jesus was raised from the dead, we've been given a brand-new life
and have everything to live for, including a future in heaven—and the
future starts now! . . .
    As obedient children, let yourselves be pulled into a way of life shaped
by God's life, a life energetic and blazing with holiness. . . .*

Your life is a journey you must travel with a deep consciousness of God.
It cost God plenty to get you out of that dead-end, empty-headed life you
grew up in. (1 Peter 1:3-4, 16, 18)

Now that you've cleaned up your lives by following the truth, love one
another as if your lives depended on it. Your new life is not like your old
life. Your old birth came from mortal sperm; your new birth comes from
God's living Word. Just think: a life conceived by God himself! That's why
the prophet said,
    The old life is a grass life,
       its beauty as short-lived as wildflowers;
    Grass dries up, flowers droop,
       God's Word goes on and on forever.
This is the Word that conceived the new life in you. (1 Peter 1:22-25)

Whoever wants to embrace life
    and see the day fill up with good,
Here's what you do:
    Say nothing evil or hurtful;
Snub evil and cultivate good;
    run after peace for all you're worth.
God looks on all this with approval. (1 Peter 3:10-12)

Dear friends, I've dropped everything to write you about this life of
salvation that we have in common. . . .
    But you, dear friends, carefully build yourselves up in this most holy
faith by praying in the Holy Spirit, staying right at the center of God's love,
keeping your arms open and outstretched, ready for the mercy of our Master,
Jesus Christ. This is the unending life, the real life! (Jude 3, 20-21)

NOTES

Chapter 1: What If You Knew You Were Going to Live Tomorrow?

p. 29   I am indebted to Dallas Willard: I can't recall now, but I either read them in his books (his book *The Divine Conspiracy* is one of the most important books in my life) or heard them in a public talk or from him in private.

Chapter 2: Jesus' Surprising Gospel

p. 36   "Belief by its very nature requires assent": Eugene H. Peterson, *Christ Plays in Ten Thousand Places* (Grand Rapids: Eerdmans, 2005), p. 94.

p. 37   "to trust in, rely on, and cling to": from *The Amplified Bible*. For instance, Numbers 14:11; Mark 1:14-15; John 3:18; 17:20.

p. 37   Belief is "obedient participation": Peterson, *Christ Plays in Ten Thousand Places*, p. 93.

p. 39   The scene is set: N. T. Wright, *Simply Christian* (San Francisco: HarperOne, 2006), p. 186.

p. 39   "The great [religious] traditions": Krista Tippett, *Speaking of Faith* (New York: Viking, 2007), p. 99.

p. 43   When the vision of a different life: Dallas Willard's *Renovation of the Heart* has a deep and illuminating discussion of what he calls "the reliable pattern" for spiritual transformation: vision, intention and means (Colorado Springs: NavPress, 2002), see p. 85.

p. 45   Jesus had options: I am indebted to Tom Wright's writings for the insights in this paragraph. See especially *The New Testament and the People of God* (Minneapolis: Fortress, 1992); and *Jesus and the Victory of God* (Minneapolis: Fortress, 1996).

p. 47   "Spiritual transformation into Christlikeness requires": In my recollection, this definition comes from a work group led by Dallas Willard at a TACT (Theological and Cultural Thinkers) meeting, sponsored by Mission America.

Chapter 3: It's Our Life That Counts

p. 54   the mad build-up to Y2K: This was the fear that as the year 2000 approached, millions of personal and corporate computers would crash because of a particular programming glitch. The result would be widespread chaos throughout the world. Of course, the fear was not realized.

p. 55   "the real and lasting life": "Real life" and "lasting life" are ways that Eugene Peterson often translates "eternal life" in *The Message*. In so doing I think he makes a vast contribution to the new imagination of the Christian life.

Chapter 4: The Role of the Church

p. 66   "God's covenant purpose was to choose a people": N. T. Wright, *The Climax of the Covenant* (Minneapolis: Fortress, 1991), p. 256.

p. 69   "inner-journey and outer-journey": Elizabeth O'Connor recounts the story of one local church who went on these twin journeys together. Doing so, for the sake of others, they substantially changed a deeply hurting neighborhood in the Washington, D.C., area. See Elizabeth O'Connor, *Journey Inward, Journey Outward* (Washington, D.C.: Potters House Books, 1968).

Chapter 5: Cooperative Friends of Jesus

p. 77   "The text for Christian living [is] set": Eugene Peterson, *Eat This Book* (Grand Rapids: Eerdmans, 2006), p. 40.

p. 87   Let's start with some simple definitions: *Webster's New Collegiate Dictionary*, 7th ed., s.v. "tension," "intention" and "manipulation."

Chapter 6: Consistent Lives of Creative Goodness

p. 94   "[Ours] is a society suffused with the dynamics": John Stackhouse Jr., *Humble Apologetics: Defending the Faith Today* (Oxford: Oxford University Press, 2002), p. 205.

p. 100   the firemen became arsonists: N. T. Wright, *Simply Christian* (San Francisco: HarperSanFrancisco, 2006), pp. 74-75. See also *Evil and the Justice of God* (Downers Grove, Ill.: InterVarsity Press, 2006), pp. 53ff.

p. 106   Dallas Willard on "the still small voice": Dallas Willard, *Hearing God* (Downers Grove, Ill.: InterVarsity Press, 1999), p. 117.

p. 106   "The visible world daily bludgeons us": Ibid., p. 217.

p. 107   "God comes to us precisely in and through": Ibid., p. 102.

p. 107   "He can approach our conscious life": Ibid.

p. 107   "God will not compete for our attention": Ibid., p. 90.

p. 107   "God's spiritual invasions into human life": Ibid., p. 218.

p. 107   "We are hindered in our progress": Ibid.

p. 107   Our apprenticeship to Jesus must focus: Ibid., p. 283.

p. 108   "if we restrict our discipleship": Dallas Willard, *The Divine Conspiracy* (New York: HarperSanFrancisco, 1998), p. 287.

Chapter 7: For the Sake of Others

p. 111   "Jesus is lifted up to draw us": N. T. Wright, *Following Jesus: Biblical Reflections on Discipleship* (Grand Rapids: Eerdmans, 1997), p. 40.

p. 113   "we are noted for nagging [society]": See the research of David Kinnaman in *Un-Christian* (Grand Rapids: Baker, 2007).

p. 113   "The context of all virtue in the great religious traditions": Krista Tippett, *Speaking of Faith* (New York: Penguin, 2008), p. 12.

p. 114   "Lies cannot nourish or protect you": Anne Lamott, *Grace (Eventually)* (New York: Riverhead, 2008), p. 74.

p. 117   "Many of those outside of Christianity": Kinnaman, *Un-Christian*, p. 11.

p. 117   "[The] most common reaction to the faith": Ibid., p. 15.

p. 117   "The growing hostility toward Christians": Ibid., p. 26.

p. 117   "It is important to realize that young outsiders": Ibid., p. 31.

p. 117   "Many of these young people actually": Ibid., p. 78.

p. 119   On music being of the devil: See, for example, Bob Larson's out-of-print book *The Day the Music Died* (Lake Mary, Fla.: Creation House, 1972), and Larry Norman's response in the song "Why Should the Devil Have All the Good Music?"

p. 120   "twenty million *sincere believers*": George Barna, *Revolution* (Wheaton, Ill.: Tyndale House, 2005), p. 13.

p. 121   "Though Israel's notion of God was unique": John Bright, *A History of Israel*, 3rd ed. (Philadelphia: Westminster Press, 1981), p. 148, emphasis added.

p. 121   "Through [God's] covenant with Israel": William J. Dumbrell, "Covenant," *New Dictionary of Christian Ethics and Pastoral Theology*, ed. David J. Atkinson and David H. Field (Downers Grove, Ill.: InterVarsity Press, 1995), pp. 266-67.

p. 121   "humankind stands with a more generalized covenant relationship": Ibid.

p. 121   The covenant with Adam and Eve: I am using the term *covenant* here somewhat loosely.

p. 122   Israel is a missionary people: See Darrell Guder, *Missional Church* (Grand Rapids: Eerdmans, 1998), p. 4. Guder says, "God's mission began with the call of Israel to receive God's blessings in order to be a blessing to the nations."

p. 122   Through the new covenant people find their rightful place as God's renewed humanity: N. T. Wright, *The Challenge of Jesus* (Downers Grove, Ill.: InterVarsity Press, 1999), p. 193. Wright asserts, "We will in turn be for the world not only what Jesus was for Israel but what YHWH was and is for the Israel and the world. If you believe in the presence and power of the Holy Spirit in your life, this is what it means. You are called to be truly human, but it is nothing short of the life of God within you that enables you to do so, to be remade in God's image." ·

p. 123   Second, I told them I try to be oriented to others: See Jean-Pierre de Caussade's *The Sacrament of the Present Moment* (San Francisco: HarperSanFrancisco, 1989).

Chapter 8: Through the Power of the Holy Spirit

p. 127   Alpha conference: For information on the Alpha Course, see www.alpha .org.

p. 133   Gordon Fee on the "greater gifts": Gordon Fee, *The First Epistle to the Corinthians* (Grand Rapids: Eerdmans, 1987), p. 625.

p. 133   "Be Naturally Supernatural": I learned this phrase from John Wimber.

p. 134   "The Gospel of the kingdom of God": Ray S. Anderson, *An Emerging Theology for the Emerging Church* (Downers Grove, Ill.: InterVarsity Press, 2006), pp. 112-13.

p. 134   "[Jesus] called [us] to work out [our] salvation": Ibid., p. 96.

p. 136   "Dial Down Emotions": I owe this insight to John Wimber who noticed that biblical texts recounting healing often were preceded by taking measures to calm the situation.

p. 139   A simple pattern to use in starting a divine appointment: I've updated this from a pattern taught to me by John Wimber in the early 1980s. See his discussion of it in *Power Healing* (New York: HarperOne, 1991), p. 199ff.

p. 141   Gordon Smith on conversion: Gordon T. Smith, *Beginning Well* (Downers Grove, Ill.: InterVarsity Press, 2001), p. 115.

Chapter 9: Inviting Others to Live a New Way

p. 145   To love is "to will the good of others": I owe this insight to Dallas Willard, and the private conversations we've had or the talks I've heard him give.

p. 146   "One morning I went to the back door": Devern F. Fromke, *The Ultimate Intention* (n.p.: Sure Foundation, 1999), p. 38.

p. 151   "Those who think that the cultivation": Dallas Willard, *The Great Omission: Rediscovering Jesus' Essential Teachings on Discipleship* (San Francisco: HarperSanFrancisco, 2006), p. 228.

p. 151   "Sometimes I think we've advanced": Larry Norman, "Déjà vu Medley," *In Another Land* (Solid Rock Music, 1975).

p. 155   "The Spirit is the Continuator": I owe this neologism to my friend Dr. Winn Griffin, *God's Epic Adventure: Changing the Culture by the Stories We Live and Tell* (Woodinville, Wash.: Harmon Press, 2007), p. 281.

Chapter 10: Three Is Enough Groups

p. 157 "Three Is Enough (TIE) Groups": I owe thanks to my friend Barb Henderson for the name "Three Is Enough.

p. 161 *The Fall of the Evangelical Nation*: Christine Wicker, *The Fall of the Evangelical Nation* (New York: HarperOne, 2008), p. ix.

p. 161 The evangelical version of Christianity: Ibid., p. 123.

p. 161 they are leaving out of deep, Bible-inspired values: Ibid., p. 125.

p. 161 Twenty million believers are now: Ibid., p. xiii.

p. 161 They outnumber evangelicals: Ibid., p. 53.

p. 161 Only prostitutes ranked lower: Ibid., p. 143.

pp. 168-70 E-mail from a TIE group member to Todd: The names in this e-mail have been changed.

Appendix 1

p. 173 Cursillo movement. For information on the movement see www.natl-cursillo.org/whatis.html.

p. 173 "A Brief History of Triads": Robert E. Logan and Sherilyn Carlton, *Coaching 101* (St. Charles, Ill.: ChurchSmart Resources, 2003), pp. 112-13.